WHEN MEMORY COMES

ALSO BY SAUL FRIEDLÄNDER

When Memory Comes: The Later Years

Franz Kafka: The Poet of Shame and Guilt

Nazi Germany and the Jews, 1933–1945 (Abridged Edition)

The Years of Extermination: Nazi Germany and the Jews, 1939–1945

Nazi Germany and the Jews: The Years of Persecution, 1933–1939

Memory, History, and the Extermination of the Jews of Europe

*Probing the Limits of Representation: Nazism and the
"Final Solution"* (editor)

Visions of Apocalypse: End or Rebirth? (co-editor)

When Memory Comes

Saul Friedländer

TRANSLATED FROM THE FRENCH BY
Helen R. Lane

WITH AN INTRODUCTION BY
Claire Messud

Other Press
New York

Production editor: Yvonne E. Cárdenas
Text designer: Julie Fry
This book was set in Fournier by Alpha Design & Composition
of Pittsfield, NH

10 9 8 7 6 5 4 3 2 1

Library of Congress Cataloging-in-Publication Data

Names: Friedländer, Saul, 1932- author. | Lane, Helen R., translator.
Title: When memory comes / by Saul Friedländer ; translated from the
French by Helen R. Lane ; with an introduction by Claire Messud.
Other titles: Quand vient le souvenir— . English
Description: New York : Other Press, [2016] | ?1979 | Originally pub-
lished: 1st ed. New York : Farrar, Straus, Giroux, 1979.
Identifiers: LCCN 2016003710 (print) | LCCN 2016005051 (ebook) |
ISBN 9781590518076 (hardcover) | ISBN 9781590518083 (e-book)
Subjects: LCSH: Friedländer, Saul, 1932- | Jews—France—Biography.
| Holocaust, Jewish (1939-1945)—France—Personal narratives. |
France—Biography.
Classification: LCC DS135.F9 F74513 2016 (print) | LCC DS135.F9
(ebook) | DDC 940.53/18092—dc23
LC record available at http://lccn.loc.gov/2016003710

For Eli, David, and Michal,
and for Hagith,
who has always understood

When knowledge comes, memory comes too, little by little. Knowledge and memory are one and the same thing.

—Gustav Meyrink

INTRODUCTION

by Claire Messud

We have understood, at least since Aeschylus, that wisdom is attained through suffering. But it is a truth powerfully reinforced by the experiences of Saul Friedländer's generation: born into a prosperous, assimilated Jewish family in Prague in 1932, Friedländer had experienced by the age of sixteen more trauma, upheaval, and grief than many do in a lifetime. This memoir of his youth, written in a moment of comparative hope (at the time of Anwar Sadat's visit to Israel in 1977, in the run-up to the Camp David Accords of 1978), is valuable not simply for Friedländer's inspiringly vivid and elegant account of his youthful travails, but also for his Tiresian clarity of vision, and for the forthrightness of his narrative. It is, if anything, only more relevant forty years after its initial publication.

Few have inhabited such diverse personae as did the young Friedländer: born Pavel, a Czech boy, he became "Paul" when his family fled to France in 1939, settling in Néris les Bains, "Vichy on a smaller scale minus the government plus the Jews." Subsequently, placed in a Jesuit boarding school, Saint-Béranger, by his parents (who would themselves die in Auschwitz), he was known as "Paul-Henri Ferland." Immediately after the war, having come to understand for the first time his Jewish identity, he was sent to a Russian-Jewish guardian in Paris, where he attended the Lycée Henri IV. From there, in the spring of 1948, he ran away to join Betar, "a youth movement with ties to Menachem Begin's Irgun." As a new Israeli, he took the Hebrew name "Shaul," the French transliteration of which is Saul.

Internal confusion was inevitable along his journey, as was a sense of isolation. As a teenager, he refused meat at his first Passover Seder because it was Good Friday. Of his Catholic years at Saint-Béranger, he recalls that, unaware of his Jewishness, "I soon felt a vocation: I wanted to become a priest"; "I liked the austere simplicity, the intense devotion of the early mass at which I sometimes served." He remembers, too, being part of the school's majority, "faithful to the Marshal [Pétain] in every way," that ostracized a young boy named Jean-Marc on account of his Gaullist views: "how happy I was to be able to share this fraternal warmth and look upon this proscribed youngster with scornful eyes!" Even in midlife, he acknowledges that "I still feel a strange attraction, mingled with a profound repulsion, for this phase of my childhood."

From this unlikely extreme, with the revelation of his heritage and of his parents' fates, he turned, in 1947–1948, to fervent Zionism. As he abandoned his French schooling and his known world, he did so for reasons not wholly dissimilar to those behind his earlier enthusiastic embrace of Catholicism: "I was all alone in the world . . . To leave for Eretz [Israel] meant merging my personal fate with a common lot, and also a dream of communion and community." Ultimately, an unmitigated sense of belonging would continue to elude Friedländer as an adult, and it is this very not-belonging that affords him so rare and crucial a perspective.

He recalls a moment when, as a newly Jewish-identified teenager, he sought to conjure imaginatively an experience of the camps Belzec and Maidanek (which of course he had not seen):

It was only much later . . . that I understood that what was missing was not literary talent but rather a certain ability to identify. The veil between events and me had not been rent. I had lived on the edges of catastrophe; a distance —impassable, perhaps— separated me from those who had been directly caught up in the tide of events, and despite all my efforts, I remained, in my own eyes, not so much a victim as—a spectator. I was destined, therefore, to wander among several worlds, knowing them, understanding them—better, perhaps, than many others—but nonetheless incapable of feeling an identification without any reticence, incapable of seeing, understanding, and belonging in a single, immediate, total movement. Hence—need I say?—my enormous difficulty in writing this book.

Seeking in part to rend the veil, in part to understand his past—having fruitlessly attempted a Proustian conjuring with a strawberry milkshake in the Paris milk bar he'd frequented with his mother as a small boy: "though it brings back memories, [it] doesn't summon up what I am looking for . . . No, really not . . ."—Friedländer turned, with ardor, to history. The memoir's title is the inversion of a quotation from Gustav Meyrink (author of *The Golem*, an Austrian writer and Prague resident who died in the year of Friedländer's birth): Meyrink wrote that "When knowledge comes, memory comes too"; for Friedländer, in life's path of self-discovery, "when memory comes, knowledge comes too."

The essential and abiding lesson is that "Knowledge and memory are one and the same thing." To bear witness to his multiple, incongruent selves amounts, for Friedländer, to acknowledging the experiences of others, whether they are fellow Jews or Palestinians or his Czech nanny Vlasta, who went on to work for the family of a German general. He has had the fortitude to examine clearly even the acts of the Nazis themselves. To bear witness is to recognize, in his young daughter's face, the echo of his lost mother's; or simply to evoke, with magnificent Tolstoyan precision, the details of a distant memory:

> *I must have been no more than three and . . . [my grandmother Cécile] was busy at the stove. I could hear her talking, I could hear the little repeated sounds of a wooden spoon tapping the sides of a pot and in the background the noise of flies circling the immense table; from time to time a brief silence announced that one of them had just gotten stuck on the ribbon of yellow flypaper, already studded with black dots, which hung from one of the beams overhead.*

In a moment of self-doubt, Friedländer asks, "what are the values that I myself can transmit? Can experience as personal, as contradictory as mine rouse an echo here, in even the most indirect way?" The answer, unreservedly, is yes. Friedländer's incapacity wholeheartedly and unthinkingly to "identify" is also his great gift. His liminal sensibility has enabled him, as a historian of the Nazi era, to seek out truths in their full horror and in their nuanced complexity; and as a citizen of Israel, to speak out for dialogue and justice even when—especially when—these calls have been unpopular. He records too the moments when, as with the young Jean-Marc in boarding school, he did not speak out, and has compassion for those failures also. That he sees the gamut of perspectives enables him to write, and to think, without vanity or superiority. A priori, to be aware of the "enormous difficulty in writing this book" is to insist upon a truthfulness that is all too rare.

Much has changed since Friedländer wrote *When Memory Comes*, as becomes clear in its powerful new companion volume, *Where Memory Leads*; and yet inevitably, much has remained the same. Contemporary culture's apparent unwillingness to embrace memory, and with it knowledge, risks leading us anew down dark paths. Jingoism and hate-filled rhetoric threaten in Europe and the United States, stirred by demagogues of scant, or nonexistent, moral character. Even in the face of these perils, Friedländer—the outsider who has chosen to embrace community—offers perspective and an individual course of action:

> *It took me a long time . . . to admit that a living community follows paths that are often impossible to predict and map out in advance, that dilemmas and contradictions are part of this journey, that at best the role of each individual remains to affirm certain principles that are essential to him, in an attempt to erect dikes along the shores, and guardrails along the edges of history.*

Edgar's words at the close of King Lear come inevitably to mind: "We that are young / Shall never see so much, nor live so long" [Act V, Scene 3]. But just as Friedländer inverts Meyrink's words, so too his book plays upon Shakespeare's: in youth, he had already seen so much. And through his testimony, those experiences, and the wisdom born of them, will live on, hopefully for a long time.

Claire Messud
Cambridge, Massachusetts
June 2016

Part I

I was born in Prague at the worst possible moment, four months before Hitler came to power. My father was also born in Prague, while my mother came from the Sudetenland, from Rochlitz, a little textile town near Gablonz celebrated for its glassware. My maternal grandfather, Gustav Glaser, had set up a factory in Rochlitz that soon became unusually successful, thanks to a simple idea.

He had behind him a career as a schoolteacher — a very rare attainment for a Jew from the Sudetenland — that was to lead indirectly to his making a fortune. He had witnessed the miserable lot of sewing teachers in Austro-Hungarian elementary schools, who were obliged to furnish all the cloth needed in their classes themselves. Once his factory had been set up, my grandfather went to see some of them, in Rochlitz, Gablonz, and other neighboring towns, with a proposal: in exchange for remnants that would be useful in their sewing classes, they would act as unofficial representatives of the new firm. Success soon followed. In a few years' time, most sewing teachers in the Austro-Hungarian Empire had become representatives of Gustav Glaser textiles: tablecloths and napkins with the initials GG woven into the cloth could be found from the Carpathians to the Adige.

This story serves to illustrate a certain Jewish ingenuity that, as everyone knows, aroused formidable hatred. Some Jews, it is true, were less honest, and others less ingenious than my grandfather, yet he is fairly representative of a certain type of minor Jewish industrialist at the beginning of the century. One may well wonder, however, whether it might not have been for his good and that of all his people if they had had less imagination.

Jewish ingenuity did nothing to change the fact that everyone in our house felt German. Shall I cite an example of this "Germanness"? Like all the children of our class, I was unable to escape piano lessons, though they were given to me by members of the family. The first song I was taught to play — and the only one I remember — was "Ich hatt' einen Kameraden": a funeral march, the one most often played in the German army and one performed at great ceremonial occasions during the Third Reich.

I have often thought about this recently, and perhaps understand the attachment of my family to things German. Both my father and my maternal uncle had served during the First World War as artillery officers in the Austro-Hungarian army; that was how they met each other and how my father came to know Elli Glaser, my mother. It may well be that for my father, as for my uncle and for tens of thousands of other Jewish veterans of the German and Austrian armies, "Ich hatt' einen Kameraden" expressed first and foremost the feeling of a certain brotherhood in arms that they had (as yet) been unable to overcome. And also — strange as it may seem — the marvelous kitsch of German military melodies has an almost spellbinding quality; the product of a nation's love for music, they have an effect on behavior that has yet to be studied in depth.

For these first years of my life, my mother remains less vivid in my memory than my father, who from the beginning appeared to me to be an extraordinary person, doubtless because I saw him through a child's eyes, but also because he kept his distance from all of us. The total upheaval that was soon to come did not change my original image of him at all, and when I think of him I quite naturally see in my mind's eye the reserved figure of this early period in my life.

Although he was born in Prague, my father spent several years with an uncle in Lemberg, in Galicia; it was there that he completed his secondary studies. I deduce from this that he was familiar, for a time at least, with a Jewish milieu that was still Orthodox for the most part; yet he bore no apparent traces of such a background.

On returning to Prague, he hesitated between law school and the conservatory, for he was a very good pianist. I can still see him leaning over the grand piano playing some transcription of Wagner, some piece by Chopin — the latter was the name engraved on the personal book plates in his library. My father seems to have had two passions: music and books. He chose law and insurance, however, and later became vice president of a large German insurance company in Czechoslovakia. A bourgeois aesthete perched on the edge of a volcano, he foresaw nothing of what the future would bring.

My father's reserve no doubt concealed extreme timidity. In any case, he did not have the slightest idea of how to approach me. I have been told that for my fifth birthday he went into a toy store and ordered ten kilos of toys suitable for a five-year-old child. He showed me no signs of tenderness that I can remember during our life in Prague. In the years that followed, a different tie was created between us, but I will always regret not having had enough

5

naturalness and spontaneity as a child to take the initiative, leap up onto my father's lap, and throw my arms around his neck.

I sometimes wonder, above all, how my father experienced his Jewish identity. There were certain signs that betrayed the fact that he was not entirely indifferent to his origins. I have just mentioned the personal *ex libris* pasted in his books. It depicted a piano, a score by Chopin, and a carpenter's square, all standing out against the Star of David, which served as the background, the foundation of all the rest. This is as clearly symbolic as anything can be, and yet in our family, if memory serves me correctly, Judaism as a religion had completely disappeared.

We observed none of the rules of life that Orthodoxy laid down, celebrated none of the holidays, respected none of the customs. I remember visiting a good many of the churches of Prague with Vlasta, my Czech governess, yet I have no memory at all of the Altneuschul, the famous synagogue, said to be the oldest in Europe, though it was very close to where we lived. Nor do I have any memory of the Jewish town hall with its clock marked with Hebrew letters and hands that turned counterclockwise (I read about all that much later), or of the Jewish cemetery, as old and as famous as the synagogue. In a word, of all this heritage I remember nothing. Or almost nothing, for at home we used a few Yiddish words, in particular *meshugge,* crazy, and *nebach,* down and out. In short, we were typical representatives of the assimilated Jewish bourgeoisie of Central Europe.

In Israel I found — and still find today — almost nothing of this very special Judaism that I had thus come to be familiar with. I say "almost," because on my arrival in Israel I was taken in by my uncle and lived with him in Nira, a village on the Plain of Sharon where certain traces of this atmosphere still remained. (I will speak later of my arrival, at the age of fifteen, a few weeks after the creation of the State of Israel.) I discovered there a milieu that even then struck me as being very odd.

The inhabitants of Nira, Beit Itzhak, and other villages round about had come, for the most part, from Prague, and some from a few large German cities, shortly before the Second World War. Out of thirty heads of households in Nira, at least half were "Herr Doktors." During the day they were all transformed: one might well have mistaken who they were, had it not been for the fact that they were just a bit *too* peasant, *too* unbuttoned. And there was also the language problem: their guttural accents, incomprehensible in any other context, represented, not a flight of recently acquired Biblical eloquence, but some typical Berlin speech patterns. Their German was punctuated, however, by a number of Hebrew words, the ones for chicken yard, sprinkler, tractor, or orange grove. What is more, only those practiced in Hebrew possessed this vocabulary: the majority of the inhabitants of Nira and Beit Itzhak were like good Herr Nehap, our grocer.

Herr Nehap from Hanover . . . An obese man, he moved slowly behind his counter, an eternal dead cigar stuck in the corner of his mouth, a majestic figure against a background of canned goods and jars of dill pickles. "*Shalom*, Friedländer!" he would say good-naturedly, the moment I crossed the gleaming threshold of his perfectly polished shop. And we both felt that by some miracle the *shalom* pronounced so naturally would this time be followed by a flood of Hebrew words, mysteriously stored in Herr Nehap's cerebral lobes for nearly fifteen years. But the *shalom* remained suspended for a few seconds in an expectant silence, and then, as though he had come up against some invisible inner barrier, Herr Nehap's enthusiasm would wane: his triumphant smile would grow vaguely apprehensive once more, and after the pause that had signaled linguistic conquests to come and inevitably ended in defeat, he would continue, in a discouraged tone, *"Also, wie geht's?"*

It was in the evening, after long workdays in the sun, that the world of "yesterday" came to occupy its true place once again. Over their bridge game, surrounded by the few pieces of furniture and books that still belonged to "back home," our peasants took on their real nature once more and dropped their masks, so to speak. Heller, Fleishman, Prager, or Glaser seemed to forget the mosquito bites, the drone of the sprinklers, or the smell of orange blossom, and they must all have had the impression that they were back once again in those large, rather dark apartments that I had known for such a short time, but whose scent, that discreet charm made up of old things, wax-polished wood, and well-worn leather, I can still describe today. Heller and Fleishman represented a disappearing species: it scarcely survives in Israel nowadays. Nira and Beit Itzhak are still there, but things aren't the same any more.

The way of life of the Jews in the Prague of my childhood was perhaps futile and "rootless," seen from a historical viewpoint. Yet this way of life was ours, the one we treasured, and there is no point in pretending otherwise. Its collapse was unexpected — however strange that may seem — and spectacular. But that is another episode.

June 5, 1977

The tenth anniversary of the beginning of the Six-Day War. A period of tension, anxiety, and enthusiasm. Since the war, everything is different. A powerful forward impetus is being maintained, despite obstacles; at the same time, on another level, forces of disintegration are undermining our efforts. Israel: country of every possible contradiction and every possible paradox.

I lived through these events with fervor, and when I began teaching in Jerusalem, in the fall of 1967, everything seemed new and wondrous to me, as it had when I arrived in Israel for the first time almost twenty years before. What was my strongest impression during this decisive year? Perhaps the one made on me by a certain category of students: the "soldier-intellectuals." Bearers of the nation's destiny, hallowed, and thereby glorified, by their permanent contact with death, young people thirsting for knowledge — that was how they struck me, and in a way that is what they were. Other places and other times have borne the imprint of young people of this sort: those back from a battlefront, and soon to return to it, sitting leaning against a tank to read a poem or a page of philosophy. It is one of the most moving images of our time, created by a reality that no longer exists — except, of course, right here, in Israel

How can I describe my enthusiasm when I first arrived in Israel during the War of Independence? Everything seemed a miracle to me: the local chocolate quite as much as the Jewish state itself.

I began by talking about the people in Nira, but I should also describe the village. The bus from Natanya deposited you in front of a little textile factory with ocher walls, which, before my arrival, produced cotton goods, and afterward was converted for the production of camouflage nets for our nascent army.

The houses of Nira were all alike, and had been built, I believe, shortly before the Second World War: little square houses with white walls, topped by red tile roofs, which stood out against the dark green background of the orange groves. Climbing plants on the walls added brighter, ever-changing colors according to the season: wisteria, honeysuckle, and sometimes, at the entrance to a garden, beds of rhododendrons.

I almost forgot the hen yards. They constituted an essential feature of the *meshek*, a word that could be translated as "farm," but meaning a modern model farm. When I say hen yard, you probably think of a poultry yard where the hens move about freely, pecking leisurely at grain. This was not at all the case in Nira. The hens were housed in cages alongside each other, forming geometric shapes, illuminated around the clock by electric lights to encourage egg laying. It was this that was responsible for the monotonous, incessant cackling which went on around us night and day.

Pleasures in Nira, in Beit Itzhak, in the villages of the plain were simple ones. Apart from the evenings playing bridge, the most enjoyable thing at the end of a long day in the sun was to meet in the café that overlooked all the surrounding countryside, beneath the water tower of Beit ltzhak, summon "Herr Ober," order a beer, and watch the slow approach of darkness, as the lights of Natanya went on one by one along the line of dunes.

On Friday evenings we went to the movies at Shaar Hefer, a neighboring village. The benches were set out in rows beneath two eucalyptus trees in front of the door of the grocery store. The screen was put in place, Herr Cohen set up the projector, and the show would begin, punctuated by breakdowns and interruptions that bothered no one: in the heat of those nights, there was at least as much hugging and kissing on the benches in front of Shaar Hefer's grocery store as in the heart-throbbing melodramas that reached us at the end of their run.

After several months in Nira, I became a boarder at an agricultural center for the education of newcomers which hugged the sea near Natanya. There I learned Hebrew and discovered the rudiments of a Jewish culture entirely new to me.

That year, most of the boarders at Ben Shemen came from Bulgaria, bringing with them all the charm of a prosperous Sephardic community that on the whole had been spared the lot of the Jewish communities in North Africa and the Middle East. Our daily life unfolded amid general gaiety, which reached its climax in the interminable horas we danced every night, and in the Bulgarian songs celebrating the Valley of Maritza — all this a few hundred meters from a very gentle sea, beneath a sky sparkling with stars.

Learning Hebrew meant, above all, discovering the Bible. The Bible soon fascinated me, and the simplest passages we read were perhaps those that bore the most powerful message, that were infused with the most intense poetry. For me, for example, who had changed my name from Paul to Shaul (Saul) upon arriving in the country, the story of this first king of Israel, told in the Book of Samuel with so much controlled force, became the very image of the tragic: called against his will, and then abandoned by all, even by God, who refuses to answer, Shaul on the eve of his greatest trial is reduced to resorting to necromancy, learning his destiny from the witch of Endor.

Along with the Bible, we also discovered Jewish life at the beginning of the century, the life that had flowered in Eastern Europe. The typical tiny Jewish village in Russia came alive for us through the stories of I. L. Peretz and Sholem Aleichem. They may not be great literature, but they have all the warmth and flavor of an authentic tradition.

Should I confess that from the beginning I nonetheless had vague, confused, intermittent feelings that something was missing? From time to time I would go sit on the beach behind a sandy rock and open a book that was merely a symbol — Fromentin's *Dominique*, in one instance that occurs to me. I thought that I was thus affirming, for myself alone, the permanence of a culture that remained the only one that mattered in my eyes. This was a slight premonition of future dilemmas, though entirely eclipsed by another habit of mine, equally harmless but much more indicative of my state of mind at this time. At midday we students had a two- or three-hour recess on account of the heat. Every day, after the noon meal, I would start out for Natanya along the beach (the shortest route, but also the one least sheltered from the sun), all alone and almost running, to buy the daily paper — which I could barely understand — and take pleasure in the announcement in it of some feat of valor, some new victory, or simply in its accounts of the everyday life of the country. Yes, I was insatiable, and the most trivial news story filled me with joy: a stretch of road had just been inaugurated here or there; this or that many kilometers of irrigation pipe had been laid; in short, Israel lived (as a Hasidic song has it), and I could see the miracle taking place before my very eyes, on pages I had deciphered slowly, but with that much more pleasure for so doing.

When did I feel the first tremors of what was going on around me — when did I feel the stable and peaceful world of my earliest years begin to shift? I could not say exactly, for I think the inner upheavals that preceded the events that made history were later integrated with these latter to form an indissoluble whole. Inner upheavals: the fear of being abandoned, and successive encounters with death.

The fear of being abandoned: I am unable to account for its deepest origins, but a "screen image" will suffice to demonstrate its intensity. A scene, always the same one, that in some way sums up for me the essence of this period: I see my father once again, in the living room, reading beneath the light of a tall standing lamp, the library in the background. This was how I saw him almost every night when there were no guests for dinner, when

I therefore heard no sounds and hence, moved by an absolutely uncontrollable anxiety, I would get up out of bed, tiptoe along the hall, and assure myself by pressing my eye to the keyhole that he was there, in his usual place.

A child of five who starts across the Charles Bridge with Vlasta, and suddenly hears crashing metal, screeching sounds, and screams, and sees, before Vlasta has time to put her hands over his eyes, a body cut in half by the wheels of a streetcar, understands the meaning of death. Moreover, a strange memory of this event haunts me. After the accident we crossed the bridge and took the path through Hradčany Park, as we did every day. We took the same route on our way home, but by then it was at least two or three hours later. I am unable to explain how or why, but at the end of this same bridge a small crowd had gathered. This nonetheless did not prevent me from seeing something shapeless, covered with a piece of canvas, near the parapet. Vlasta told me that it was the dead body of the victim of the accident, and that is also what I gathered from the remarks of the throng of morbid bystanders . . . This is impossible, isn't it? An obvious fantasy that shows how forcibly the accident had affected my imagination.

But it was about a year later that death made an even more lasting impression on me, a more massive one, so to speak. I had just started school when the director, whom I had seen on the first day of classes, died suddenly. We attended the funeral, and from the beginning everything impressed me deeply: the dark clothes, the serious faces, the whispers. We entered an immense cemetery, walked alongside a wall covered with marble plaques, and went into a vast room that in my memory seems like a theater. There were chairs, and in front of us a sort of stage, where the coffin stood, surrounded by funeral wreaths of various sizes. Things I barely understood were said, and then something happened, insignificant for others present, but which remained deeply engraved on my memory: the coffin slid behind the stage on invisible rails, the lights on stage dimmed, the curtain slowly fell, and funeral music filled the room.

This strange ceremony alone would have filled me with an icy terror, but what is more, either in answer to a question from me or in an effort to keep me from imagining things, my mother or Vlasta explained to me that the director's body was going to be cremated. They told me that the metal coffin would be put in an oven where it would be heated white-hot, and this would reduce the dead body to ashes. Whether this explanation was true or not, it was the first time I had ever heard of an oven for cremating people, and I was deeply upset by it.

For a long time the director's cremation haunted my nightmares. The mind of a child interprets the world in its own way, especially when that child is aware of a growing anxiety round about him which is still, however, difficult for him to identify.

By now I should be able to speak quite naturally of the first real changes in our existence, and yet I hang back, somehow hesitating to leave this calm and, when all is said and done, happy period of my life, despite a few ominous shadows. Everyday images come back to my mind: Rochlitz again, with frost flowers in the early morning; the squeak of snow under the soles of my shoes; two dogs, the boxer Ali and Rolf the German shepherd; a pedal car; raspberry bushes — the whole dominated by a large building with windows that are narrow and higher, it seems to me, than those of the other houses. Rochlitz again: mountains with gentle slopes covered in pine forests, and — another winter image — my mother turns around, a pair of skis on her shoulder, slender and beautiful, with a radiant smile and a face glistening in the cold.

But it is Vlasta whom I find everywhere. I am evoking images; I should also speak of the sounds. On Sunday mornings Vlasta would take me to hear the military band at the entrance to the castle. After that we would often enter a church to hear mass, and whether it was a holiday or not, Vlasta would teach me prayers and songs . . . I can still recite two things in Czech, no more: a prayer to the Guardian Angel and the words of a song, "Po starých zámeckých schodech":

> *On the ancient stairs of the castle,*
> *On the stairs climbing upward,*
> *A girl walks each evening.*
> *She holds a boy's hand,*
> *Her heart is of marble . . .*

The influence of the Vlastas of all nationalities on the rapid assimilation of the Jewish bourgeoisie of Europe merits study. The Vlastas formed, quite naturally, the essential link between the Jewish child and the world around him.

Though prayers and churches might pose a problem, what could be simpler than to sympathize with the sufferings of the boy whose friend had a heart of marble, to hear the military band, or to spend long moments in one of the food shops in the Old City? I never learned to distinguish the different animal parts on sale there, but I never tired of looking at a painting which hung above the counter, representing a furious battle — that of the White Mountain, I imagine. Day after day I followed, with the same anxiety, the motionless efforts of one of the knights, trapped under his horse, a broken sword at his side, his dying eyes open wide, his mouth contorted, as though in a last supreme cry he were endeavoring to communicate some fateful message to the customers who had come into the shop to buy a portion of sauerkraut with pork, some raw ham, and some little grilled sausages. That — and the rest — was Prague.

Whether I consciously remember it or not, I caught all the signs of this city: the most insignificant baroque town still immediately arouses in me a powerful echo that can only come from these childhood impressions. Isolated images, but precious ones, nonetheless: of streets and shop windows lighted up for the year-end festivities, the feast of Saint Nicholas, Christmas of course, and New Year's. Everyone is familiar with the "crystal" ornaments and the aluminum tinsel that shine so brightly when the shop windows light up at nightfall; well, in Prague, at the time I am speaking of, the ornaments, the tinsel, and the stars were brighter than anywhere else, the Christmas tree put up every year in front of the Church of Saint Nicholas was the most imposing of all those decorating the squares of Europe, and the wool stockings (for at our house it was wool stockings and not shoes or wooden clogs) hung up waiting for presents (on the feast of Saint Nicholas, not Christmas) turned out to be filled to the very top like nowhere else in the world.

Before the war, Prague was perhaps not the liveliest city in Europe, nor, doubtless, the most "intellectual," but it was surely the most civilized and pleasant. And it was certainly the most mysterious. Legends lived on there in their natural setting, made up of history, baroque architecture, little back streets of the Old City, and fog, the fog from the Vltava. Thus scraps of the legend of the Golem, a Prague legend, a Jewish one this time, nourished my imagination as a child.

The Golem was a robot of clay, endowed with a semblance of life, that the grand rabbi Loew, the great Maharal, created to serve the Jewish community. The robot wandered through the city dressed as a street porter, or made invisible by a magic amulet so as to sniff out the plots woven against the Jews by the Capuchin friar Thaddeus and his acolytes . . . There are countless tales surrounding the miraculous rabbi and his fantastic servant. Legend has it that the emperor Rudolph himself, fascinated by magic and the supernatural, summoned the great Kabbalist to his castle in Hradčany to converse with him of hidden things, though none of the details of this conversation ever leaked out.

The Golem's end has often been recounted, in widely varying versions. According to one of them, the robot suddenly escaped from his master's control and began raging through the ghetto in a fit of violent madness, destroying everything in his path. To breathe life into him, the Hebrew word *emeth*, "truth," written on a scrap of parchment, had been stuck to his forehead. To destroy the robot, it was necessary to efface the first letter, which left *meth*, "dead." Some variations of the legend have it that when the rabbi at last succeeded in erasing this first letter from the forehead of his mad robot, the immense mass of clay came crashing down and crushed the rabbi beneath its weight.

My own favorite version, whose symbolism is quite different, goes like this: Since the dangers threatening the Jews of Prague were no longer imminent, Rabbi Loew decided to destroy the robot. On the evening of the feast of Lag B'omer — the one that in our day is celebrated in Israel by lighting fires signaling to each other from hill to hill — he ordered the Golem to go sleep upstairs in the attic of the old synagogue. When the clock towers of the city struck two, the rabbi, preceded by a servant bearing two candles and accompanied by his son-in-law Isaac and his disciple Jacob, climbed up to the attic, where the Golem lay in a deep slumber. At the time of the creation of the robot, the rabbi and his aides had placed themselves at the feet of the clay statue stretched out on the ground and recited the magic formulas of the Sefer Yetzirah, the Kabbalist Book of Creation; this time they posted themselves behind the Golem's head and the phrases of the Sefer Yetzirah were read backward. When the last word died away, the Golem had become a mere heap of clay once more. After burning his garments in secret, they covered him with old prayer books lying about in the attic of the synagogue, and Rabbi Loew forbade all access to the place forever.

The Golem has not altogether disappeared, however: on winter nights he continues to roam the site of the ghetto, and many are those who, in the course of the centuries, have thought they caught a glimpse of his hairless face with its prominent cheekbones and slightly slanted eyes, as he hastens along with his strange stumbling gait, as though he were about to fall on his face at any moment.

Everyone interprets symbols in his own way. To me the first variation of the legend announces the fate of the Jews, sorcerer's apprentices who set in motion forces they could no longer control; and the second prefigures the essential feature of Jewish life in our time: a perpetual restlessness, an anxiety in perpetual motion.

As a child I was familiar with yet another version of the story of the Golem. My father was less interested, I think, in its Jewish content than in its esoteric meaning, the one provided him by Gustav Meyrink's strange retelling of the legend, of which he possessed a magnificent copy, illustrated by the engraver Hugo Steiner. Moreover, it was one of the rare books that he took out of Czechoslovakia with him; we often used to leaf through the rather rough-textured pages together. How many daydreams of mine are linked with this haunting, spellbinding book!

Later I read this sentence in it: "When knowledge comes, memory comes too, little by little. Knowledge and memory are one and the same thing."

2

June 26, 1977

Jerusalem turns almost violet as night falls. The roses in our garden are overblown and already fading, but dozens of new buds will soon open.

I had to go down to Tel Aviv this morning. What strikes one on arriving on the plain is the extraordinary dynamism of this country. From Ramleh on, a steady stream of heavy trucks, loaded with machines, crates, pipes, and all sorts of equipment, invades the highway; on the right a group of dwellings that was not there two months ago has sprung up out of the ground: stretching out on the left are mile after mile of orange groves, traversed by factories, military camps, warehouses, ruled off in squares by cypresses. This vitality is that of America at the end of the nineteenth century, except for the inflation here . . . Everything is constantly moving, constantly changing, constantly growing. One can ask oneself many questions as to the direction that society is taking, and I for one do ponder them; one can wonder what has become of the dream of Israel, and I often ask myself that very question, but it is impossible not to recognize the energy that overwhelms one on every hand. This living force brings with it unpredictable changes that justify one's hopes, but also one's fears.

Following my arrival in the country, I was obliged to go to Tel Aviv for some formality or other several times during my brief stay in Nira. The coastal highway did not exist then and the bus that one boarded at Natanya made a fairly long detour by way of Beit Lid, an immense transit camp for new immigrants, flanked by a military camp; Kfar Saba, which, in the course of this journey, symbolized well-established agricultural prosperity; Ramat Gan and its factories turning out canned goods and chocolate; and finally Tel Aviv, the metropolis and at that time the capital of the new state. This trip of about an hour and a half presented a sort of symbolic résumé of the adventure that Israel was embarking upon: at Beit Lid, one saw the most diverse human types climb into the bus, and it would require another pen than mine to describe these motley groups, a bit bewildered, lost even, as I was, too, in a certain way. But Kfar Saba, Ramat Gan, Tel Aviv showed one and all the way to take root and prosper.

I mention these trips for the express purpose of speaking of Tel Aviv, for when I went there I sometimes vaguely felt, as at Ben Shemen, an incompatibility — almost imperceptible, it is true, but nonetheless present and capable of suddenly mounting to the surface, like those toothaches that for a long time are mere dull reminders but can suddenly transform themselves into unbearable pain.

I was proud of Tel Aviv, as though I had erected it myself; I hastened to see its most recent buildings and was entranced by the strong pulsations of an urban life that in reality were simply those of an average city in the Middle East. I could feel the power of the effort being expended every day and the dimensions of the success achieved. Sometimes, however, the dirty peeling façades, the decrepit look of buildings only recently constructed, the glaring, naive bad taste of the store display windows, the absence of any conception of city planning, and above all the noisy vulgarity of the people, got the upper hand and even at this early point in my life aroused in me a feeling of malaise, a brief and limited one it is true, but one that nonetheless went beyond simple aesthetic sensibility and somewhere awakened in me profound misgivings that, perhaps, went to the very heart of things.

June 27, 1977

It suffices to go out just a little bit earlier in the morning than usual to see Arab workers from the occupied territories or from East Jerusalem in the streets, hurrying to work in the Jewish part of the city in an almost steady stream. On their heads are white kaffiyehs, held down with a colored cord, or a simple wool skullcap. Buses take them to the Jaffa Gate or the Damascus Gate; from there they continue on foot. Seemingly peace-loving groups, seemingly satisfied people. The city has been calm for a long time now: there have been no attacks, nothing. Simple people, poor people, peasant faces, with just the touch of a lost look in their eyes . . . Where does this general tranquillity come from? Fatalism, the attraction of money, fear?

In 1937 my mother and two of her brothers went on a cruise that took them to Palestine. The names of Tel Aviv and Haifa came back to us on postcards. At that time Tel Aviv for some reason had particular associations for me; not a city, but rather a certain taste of caramel . . .

The mention of this trip allows me to give a certain shading to what I have written about our family's relationship to Judaism. There was nothing at the level of religious tradition, certainly, but in the case of my mother and her brothers there was a more or less active interest in Zionism. The oldest brother, my Uncle Paul, was, moreover, a member of Blau-Weiss, a group of Zionist persuasion active in Germany and in Prague. He was the mentor of this expedition.

The youngest brother, my Uncle Hans, came back from this trip deeply disappointed. What had he expected to find in Palestine? I do not know, but a few years ago he spoke to me of his reservations regarding what he considered to be constant expressions of an intransigent nationalism. He had been struck by the absence of any sort of understanding of the Arab position, by the militance of even the kibbutzim, when he had expected to find a Tolstoyan, egalitarian, idealistic, pacifist society. Hence my Uncle Hans's break with Zionism and his turn to anthroposophy.

My Uncle Paul, for his part, clung to his convictions and, as will be seen, soon took the road to Palestine. As for my mother, I could not say what impression her contact with Eretz Israel made on her at the time, but probably her feelings were closer to those of Paul rather than Hans, since later on she, too, contemplated leaving for Palestine. Her third brother, Willy, was interested only in chemistry.

In 1937, in any event, it was not a question of emigrating to Palestine. We did not have a care in the world. We had just left our little house in Bubeneč and moved to a luxurious apartment on the quays of the Vltava, just opposite the castle. In short, we felt perfectly safe.

As for me, the first sign of changing times was seeing my Uncle Paul in a Czech uniform, a saber at his side, in the spring of 1938, probably during the ill-starred May mobilization. We were present at several stormy demonstrations in Rochlitz by the partisans of Henlein, the pro-Nazi leader of the Sudeten Germans; it is not so much their shouts and cries that I remember as their white socks, the sign by which they recognized each other. We hurriedly returned to Prague.

I heard one of Hitler's speeches during these feverish days. We were gathered round the radio; faces were sober. The scene itself lingered in my mind, but I also retained the memory of a raucous repetition, of a sort of alliteration that I did not succeed in placing in its proper context till the day when, as I was studying this period and reading the speech given by Hitler on September 26 of that year, I came upon the following sentences: *"An einem Tag, zehntausend Flüchtlinge, am nächsten zwanzigtausend, einen Tag später schon siebenunddreissigtausend, wieder zwei Tage später einundvierzigtausend, dann zweiundsechzigtausend, dann achtundsiebzigtausend, jetzt sind es neunzigtausend, einhundertsiebentausend, einhundertsiebenunddreissigtausend und heute zweihundertvierzehntausend . . ."* What I had heard, and could never forget, was the incantatory repetition of the word *tausend*, like the panting of some monstrous locomotive.

War seemed close at hand, but then came Munich with its few months of "respite," which for Jews were to be those of a mounting debacle. But still we did not budge. At that very moment I set off for school for the first time, a private English school. Was this in anticipation of a possible departure, or, even though the Germans had not yet arrived, because Jewish children were no longer admitted to public schools? I cannot say. In any case, I remained in the school only a few months, just time enough to have difficulties with the letter *k*, the hardest one in the alphabet, to attend the funeral of our director, and to learn that I was Jewish.

I have already spoken of our director's funeral, and the letter *k* was also not without importance at this time in my life. It is said that the founder of Hasidism, the Baal Shem-Tov, forgot everything save a single letter of the alphabet, but, by clinging to this letter, by using it as his support, he rediscovered an entire world. With the single letter *k* as my point of departure, I, too, rediscovered a world, that of school first of all, of school in times that were already uncertain, when general upheavals intermingled with daily routine and formed unusual constellations. And something else, too . . .

I started school in the month of September, only a short time before the Munich Conference. People nowadays forget that, during those few days, on the eve of the final abandonment of Czechoslovakia, war seemed imminent. In Prague, alerts followed one after the other; I remember sirens, shelters, and above all the gas masks that everyone carried about like a talisman, in a cylindrical box slung across the shoulder. I thus went about with my schoolbag on my back and my gas mask at my side. I have no idea whether these gas masks would have been effective in case of an attack, but I do remember that in our family they almost brought about the death of one of us: my Aunt Martha. Like everyone else, she tried her mask on, was unable to see how to open the breathing tube, couldn't get out of the rubber envelope, and barely escaped suffocation.

Let us return to the letter *k*. A number of things resulted from my inability to master writing it. I covered my notebook with inkblots from my glass-tipped pen and had to stay after school. These punishments obliged me to confront my father's severity, but at the same time permitted me to discover my mother's indulgence. When I was kept after school, it was not Vlasta but my father or my mother who came to take me home. When it was my father who was there at the foot of the stairs, his very silence sufficed to make me understand the ignominy of my position, without making mastery of the letter *k* any more accessible for all that. For my mother, *k*'s and being kept after school seemed to have no importance: she would take me by the hand and whisk me off to the Café Slavia, right next to the school, to have a huge cup of hot chocolate. We would sit there chatting about everything and nothing. It was then, just a few months before we were to leave Prague, that I discovered how much I loved my mother. That is why I have spoken of the letter *k*.

And finally, I also learned that I was Jewish, during a weekly class in religion. I imagine that classes such as this were held in all Czech schools at the time. That might seem to involve no problem, but for the four or five of us who were Jews it was a repeated humiliation: once a week, when the catechism teacher came into the main study hall, we were obliged to leave the room, beneath the gaze of classmates that today I suppose was either mocking or amused, but one that I distinctly remember as being attentive.

We went to join a rabbi at the end of the hall, in a sort of little nook that was more like a storeroom than an office, to hear Bible stories. The rabbi quite naturally began with the creation of the world, and after that we made rapid progress: Adam and Eve, Cain and Abel, the hapless builders of the Tower of Babel, and those who happily escaped the Flood. I couldn't say whether we listened to these stories eagerly or were bored; all I remember is having heard them. We took up the story of Abraham and the sacrifice of Isaac: "Take now thy son, thine only son Isaac, whom thou lovest, and get thee into the land of Moriah; and offer him there for a burnt offering upon one of the mountains which I will tell thee of . . ." The rabbi told us the story but didn't explain anything; Vlasta could shed only very dim light on the subject; as for my parents, Biblical questions seemed to occupy them very little at this moment, when the need to flee the country was becoming increasingly obvious. I imagined Abraham journeying into the desert, bowed down by the weight of years, with his son Isaac at his side, and behind them the donkey loaded down with the wood for the burnt offering and the sword of the sacrifice. On the third day they saw Mount Moriah looming up before them . . . Then for a long time I forgot the question raised by the awesome text, only to see it arise again later, and with what forcefulness!

Why is this one of the first stories of our people? Why was it preserved in the Bible? I have read all sorts of interpretations and explanations of it, but this text does not leave me in peace: "Take now thy son, thine only son . . . and offer him for a burnt offering . . ."

Abraham's obedience explains our entire history. Today most Jews no longer obey God's injunctions, yet they still obey the call of some mysterious destiny. Why this fidelity? In the name of what?

By March 12, 1939, it had become blindingly clear, even to us, that Hitler would occupy Czecho-Slovakia (the hyphen marked the change that had taken place in six months) at any moment. My parents decided to flee across the Hungarian border by car.

All I remember of the first part of the journey is how uncomfortable I was on a back seat piled full of suitcases that left very little room. But I have not forgotten our arrival in Brno, a town in Moravia. We came out on a sort of esplanade. There loomed up before my eyes an enormous building, a city hall or a barracks: in front of the main door two sentinels wearing the helmet that is engraved on everyone's memory. It was too late: the Germans were there already. For me, despite all the many events that were to follow, Hitler's Reich is always summed up, in one first instant, by two motionless sentinels: not faces, but two helmets.

It was already dark when we got back to Prague. The sound of motors that pervaded the city shortly thereafter did not wake me up. In the morning, the only things to be seen on the streets and the quays of the Vltava were German uniforms. From our sixth floor, we could clearly see the single-seater fighter planes that skimmed the surface of the river and then suddenly veered upward to pass above the bridges. We would have to leave again — as soon as possible.

After the Germans came, I no longer went to school, and even my walks with Vlasta came to an end. I spent my days roaming about the apartment, which was full of suitcases, and watching, through the bars of the terrace railing, the military detachments, often preceded by a band, which goose-stepped by along the quays.

Sometimes my Uncle Willy, the chemist, the one who lived in a little apartment near us, invited me to come see him. To amuse me, he mixed red and green liquids together so as to make a magic flame suddenly flare up. But my secret pleasure was to stretch out at the end of the terrace under a blanket, and tirelessly watch the movements of the blood-red flag on the edge of the roof above my head — now gently waving, now briskly fluttering — with a white circle in the middle bearing the strangely symmetrical black swastika.

The eve of our departure was marked by a scene that in my mind has remained at once more distinct and more unreal than the other events of those days. As usual, my father had remained alone in the living room after dinner. After a moment, however, he asked me to join him. The shelves of the library were already empty and the piano was draped in a white dustcover, but the tall lamp was still standing in its usual place. My father was leaning against the piano, as though he was very tired. He opened a little box and showed me a ring. "It's for you," he explained. "It will help you remember the country we're about to leave . . ."

A strange gesture, very much in the style of a certain old-fashioned romanticism. But did I really need a ring to remember? Did I need a ring to see, suddenly appearing before me, the *vodník* — an untranslatable Czech word, it seems to me, designating a creature who lives underwater — of my friend Jiří, a *vodník* whose adventures necessarily unfolded in a setting that was always sea green? Did I need a ring to remember my first, brief vision of social injustice, that winter evening as my mother and I were returning home with our arms full of things we had bought in the stores, when a child in rags in front of us began to plead plaintively, "*Mamo, párky*!" ("Mama, sausages!"), alongside the little brazier on wheels from which there rose the smell, like no other in the world, of the sausages of Prague? Did I really need a ring to still see the witch in *Snow White* pry loose the rock to crush the seven dwarfs and herself be plunged, with a terrifying howl, into the abyss? Prague and the setting of my childhood, however indistinct its outlines may have been, were imprinted on my memory forever. What became of the ring? It was no doubt turned into a few months' rent money. Might it not have been one of those "trinkets" that my father mentioned at the very end?

The real reason for our leaving the country was concealed from me. I was told that we were leaving Prague because the Germans had occupied Czechoslovakia and because we were Czech. I apparently did not notice that an essential link in this explanation was missing; it seemed altogether natural that my father should impress upon me my duty to remember Prague and our country. As for our status as Jews, we were taking it with us.

The entire family, and Vlasta too, came with us to the Wilson Station to say goodbye. Two of my uncles were leaving for

Palestine soon, and the third for Sweden, where he intended to send for my grandmother. My father's sister was going to stay behind: we never saw her again.

As the train started up, I leaned out of the window of the compartment to call to Vlasta: "From now on, I'm going to shine my shoes all by myself!"

This departure was the end of a first stage. The more time passes, the more I feel that it is there, in this earliest setting of my life, rather than in the terrible upheavals that followed, that the essential part of my self was shaped. It is banal nowadays to speak of the decisive influence of one's first years of life, yet one is continually astonished to discover how indelible the imprint of this almost forgotten phase remains.

I saw Prague again only once, in unusual circumstances. It was in the spring of 1967. A Czech translation of my book on Pius XII had just come out, and in their reviews of it the Prague newspapers had added a few biographical facts about me, since I was more or less a compatriot. It was then that a letter came to me in Geneva, the first I had ever received from Czechoslovakia: through the newspaper articles, Vlasta had found me again. A few weeks later, I was with her once more.

Her hair had turned almost white by then, of course, but apart from that, she had scarcely changed at all. We walked about Prague — for hours. I asked her to retrace with me the route we had taken on our walks together in my childhood, and that was how I once again crossed the bridge where the fatal accident had happened. But Vlasta had no memory of the corpse covered with canvas that, according to me, had lain there near the parapet. Of course: how could *she* have remembered *my* fantasies?

On reaching Bubeneč, I wanted to see our house. We rang the bell; a woman came to the door and Vlasta explained what had brought us there. Everything was in the right place, so to speak: every door, every wall, every corner. This was where my mother had appeared one night when I was sick, with a basin of hot water and compresses; that was where I slept; and here was the dining room. Even our neighbor's tree had not changed. But everything had shrunk compared to my memories: the rooms had become tiny; the garden that was almost a park in my mind turned out to be a pitiful little courtyard. As for the apartment on the quays, it had been divided up into studios, so nothing of its former layout was left.

I told Vlasta the principal details of my life since we had left Prague and she spoke to me of her troubles with the regime: since, shortly after the war, she had married a tradesman who had subsequently died, she had by law no old-age pension herself, as she had found out after putting up with the petty annoyances of a socialist bureaucracy. And what had happened to her during the Nazi years? Hadn't she had trouble after working for a Jewish family for more than seven years? No, she had even found work after that, since she was a governess with a diploma. Whom had she worked for, then? It doesn't matter, she kept saying; I insisted; she got all flustered. She had been a governess in the family of a German general . . .

Yet I found that my affection for Vlasta was as great as ever, for there is no possible link between the memory of the constant companion of my early childhood and what she revealed to me thirty years later. But even if I had learned this immediately after the war, things would doubtless have been the same, since for each of us who lived through the events of this period as children there is an impassable line of cleavage somewhere in our memories: what is on this side, close to our time, remains dark, and what is on the other side still has the intense brightness of a happy dawn — even if our powers of reason and our knowledge point to obvious links between the two periods. When one looks back to the other side of the line, an irrepressible nostalgia remains.

July 2, 1977

Late yesterday afternoon. A walk in the Old City. On my route the Montefiore windmill, with the famous philanthropist's particolored barouche on display for tourists, and then the stairs of Yemin Moshe leading down to the Valley of Hinnom with the massive ocher walls jutting out over it. As I climb up the opposite slope, hugging Mount Zion, the Dead Sea, almost imperceptible at first, becomes more clearly defined in the background beneath the violet outlines of the mountains of Moab.

I meet Hasidim dressed in their black silk caftans and their big hats with fur brims. For many of them our political stirrings mean nothing, the state means nothing. One day the Messiah will come; it matters little whether this happens tomorrow or in two thousand years. Their faith is unshakable and the essential thing is to reach the Western Wall in time for prayers. Everything else . . . An anachronistic, marginal phenomenon? I am not so sure. I have heard that a return to faith, an extreme and uncompromising faith, is becoming more pronounced in very different kinds of circles: some striking conversions have been seen even in bohemian circles in Tel Aviv.

In front of me, an Arab is carrying a skinned sheep on his back, no doubt to a nearby butcher shop. From time to time he stops and sets it down in the dust . . . Tradesmen are sitting in front of their shops, their eyes calmly following me. A strong smell of spices in the evening air. The permanence of the Jewish world, but the permanence of the Arab world, too — now face to face.

A confrontation in which everything is interwoven, a confrontation where everything ceaselessly changes, but where everything remains motionless, a confrontation made up at once of paradoxes, sudden about-faces, and age-old fidelities.

I remember a meeting in Geneva at which, several years after the Six-Day War, the positions taken by the two sides were debated at length. I presented the point of view of Israel; there was not a single Arab at the table, since I, an Israeli, was present. But there were Arabs in the audience, many of them, listening intently. I addressed the audience: "It strikes me as significant and tragic that the presence of an Israeli should be reason to exclude that of an Arab. I know that there are Arabs listening to me in this hall. Isn't there one of you who will dare stand up, come up here on the platform, and hold a dialogue with me, hold a dialogue with an Israeli?"

Hesitation, suspense, and then a young man slowly rises to his feet: "I am an Arab, a Palestinian from Ramallah, and I am coming up onto the platform to speak with you. My name is Fuad Haled."

We were all moved. Something had just happened, something revealing perhaps.

Fuad Haled appeared to be a man of great discernment and sensitivity. He knew all about life in Israel and many things about Jewish history as well: he spoke of the Second World War, extermination, the Warsaw ghetto. A flame seemed to be devouring this Palestinian, and everyone present had the feeling that here was a beginning of possible contact, a first step toward brotherhood.

We saw each other again briefly that night at the home of mutual friends, but Fuad was obliged to leave soon afterward. I was then told by those present that he had introduced himself at the meeting under a pseudonym, that he was a poet and very ill, suffering from leukemia. Thus the man who seemed to be willing to stretch a hand out to us was perhaps doomed to die soon.

Two years went by and the murder of Israeli athletes at the Olympic Games in Munich suddenly took place. That very evening, a friend telephoned me: "Do you remember Fuad Haled? He died a few months ago. His real name was Fuad Shamali. He was one of the organizers of the Black September movement, one of the brains behind the Munich massacre."

Here is the Zion Gate. I turn my back on the Armenian quarter and descend, hugging the inner face of the battlements, toward the esplanade of the Western Wall; towering above it are the gold cupola of the Mosque of Omar and the silver one of al-Aksa, which the darkness is already blending into one and the same imprecise tone as it falls.

There are fewer tourists at this hour and from the stairs on which I am sitting above the esplanade the monotonous rhythm of prayers can be distinctly heard. Then a second sound in the background mingles with it, indistinct in the beginning, then more pronounced as the chanting in the foreground dies down a bit: it is the sound of hundreds of voices mounting, beyond the walls, from the Arab villages in the Valley of Siloam, like the piping of a multitude of children playing somewhere far off in the dusk.

Early in the morning we crossed the bridge at Kehl and the Rhine, still shrouded in fog. A few minutes later we entered the Strasbourg Station. For the first time, I saw round képis and berets pulled down over one ear: so we were saved.

I shall never forget crossing the "frontier" between the Czech Protectorate and the Reich. Four men came to search everything, down to my schoolbag and my pencil box; they even unscrewed my glass-tipped pen. The smell of their leather overcoats! The train finally started up again and I fell asleep. When I think of it now, I wonder how my parents spent that night. Stations and stops: Nuremberg, Stuttgart. Did Germans enter the compartment? Did they realize who we were? What sort of look did they have in their eyes, what did they say, how did they act?

Paris: the strange smell of the Gare de l'Est, the Métro, the long loaves of bread. To a child, great turning points are often reduced to such very simple differences. The first sentence I ever spoke in French, for example, learned by heart for the grocery store next door to the Hôtel Montholon, was *"Je voudrais une boîte d'allumettes, s'il vous plaît."*

Paris and its fears, at once old and new: my parents think that I am going to go quietly to sleep, as a child of my age ought to, but they forget that I am upset, worried in this new setting, and also forget that the feeling of being abandoned can pass through the protective wall of sleep, enter by way of the gates of dreams, and warn me that danger is present, a symbolic one but at the same time a certain one. I awaken in a panic. Everything in this room is new, odd, even terrifying, and my parents are gone. From the empty landing, I see the entry hall of the hotel, all lighted up, and the night clerk behind his desk. I make my way downstairs, sobbing, and try to say something to this man in the threadbare coat. How could he have understood? But the city in these days is full of emigrants and the night clerk is Polish, and doubtless Jewish; he understands and reassures me — a little. My sobs cease, we speak a mixture of Czech and Polish that reestablishes a mutual understanding that had long since disappeared between Czechs and Poles, and my parents finally come back. This must not happen again, they decide. From this time on, we were to go to the movies, to the opera, everywhere together.

That was how I came to see *La Charrette fantôme* (*The Phantom Tumbril*). I can still hear the sinister creak of the wheels that announces death and see Louis Jouvet, the ill-omened carter, outlined against the sky. I also discovered those special glasses, reddish ones as I remember, distributed at the door of movie houses, that made one see everything in the film in three dimensions. This sensation is fine when the movie is funny, but I remember the terrifying effect on me of a film describing the beginnings of aviation: I could see one of the planes crash and burst into flames as though I were present at the scene, as the body of the pilot, ejected from the fuselage, rolled inertly to the bottom of a hill . . . I was also fascinated by the final scene of *Aida* at the Opéra. The elephants had not impressed me, but a question remained in my mind: how did Aida and Radamès get out of their tomb once they had been shut up inside it?

Paris was also the shiny, lacquered, sumptuous shells of lobsters and sea crayfish that I had never seen in Prague, artfully displayed in the stalls along the rue des Martyrs; it was the spring air in Montmartre; it was the ornamental basins in the Tuileries; it was above all — my most intense memory, which later was to come to symbolize happiness to me — the taste of strawberry milk shakes, the milk shakes I drank with my mother, perched on a high, high stool in a milk bar on the boulevard des Italiens.

"Above all, don't allow yourself to be depressed by dark thoughts," my mother wrote to a woman friend who had emigrated to London.

Everyone gives in to his feelings at the beginning, and afterward one perceives that this was the wrong thing to do, that it is possible to be satisfied. One must not cling to the present, but constantly think of the future . . . Don't be resentful of my preaching; since, when all

*is said and done, I am in a situation similar to yours, I have the
right to do so, haven't I? Note that I say similar and not identical,
for I am convinced that in the beginning especially, things are easier
here. First of all, everything appears to be less expensive, and sec-
ondly, the French — and Paris — are warmer. The first days were
hard for us, too: we lived in a miserable place and I had the same
thoughts as you. Two weeks ago we found a passable place to live, in
a house furnished in the American style, with two tiny bedrooms and
a tiny kitchen: for France it is clean, modern, and cheap. We pay
350 francs a month for the apartment and since, naturally, I do all
the cooking and laundry myself, we get by on 1,500 francs a month
at the very most.*

My father soon wrote this same woman friend in London:

*For the moment, we are finding it very hard to obtain an exten-
sion of our residence permit in Paris, since in principle all immigrants
must settle in the provinces. But perhaps one fact will be in our favor:
I have been taking an electrician's course for some time, against my
will, I confess, and hence without much success, while Elli is studying
to be a beautician. Our projects, as far as Palestine is concerned, are
not getting us anywhere at all; I am waiting for papers from Prague
that haven't turned up yet and the English consul is demanding documents that I can't furnish him.*

*From time to time I meet people from Prague; many of them are
poor, and some of them are rich. Those who are here would like to
return, whereas those who are there would like to leave: they are right
in both cases.*

During the summer, in another letter, my father was more
explicit:

*You will be leaving soon for America and your situation is there-
fore better than that of hundreds of thousands of your companions in
misery, for whom the promised land is now a thing of the past. I think
that those of us who have already reached middle age will never see
our beautiful country again.*

*Three days ago the 150th anniversary of the storming of the Bas-
tille was celebrated here, with unbelievable pomp and ceremony. The
tanks and the cannon that we had waited for in vain last September
paraded down the Champs-Elysées; thousands and tens of thousands
of people sang "Le jour de gloire est arrivé . . ." There was dancing
in the streets, and the Good Lord in France put on his finest garments.*

*I have just learned that Karl's boat has reached the Syrian coast
and that everyone is in good health. The English appear to have
declared themselves ready to allow this ship to disembark its passengers, who are to be subtracted from the quota of immigration certifi-
cates, but the captain wants to avoid the seizure of the vessel that this
illegal disembarkation would result in. In any case, the arrival of Sinbad the Sailor is expected in the next few days.*

*Although the news coming out of Palestine is not very favorable as
regards the possibilities of work and the economic and social situation
of the country, everyone agrees that one has the feeling of being at
home there, as a free citizen. We can all appreciate what that means
today. I don't want to begin the same comedy all over again in another
state or in another country and would rather remain a* schnorrer *all
my life, or wage war on the Arabs. But it will be a year at best before
our turn for an immigration certificate comes up, and for people like
us there is no way to decide things so far ahead.*

*As you can readily imagine, we are not living in a bed of roses. We
have little money and are not earning any at all. That doesn't mean
that I am sitting around waiting for death, not ours at any event. We
must manage to survive.*

I translated and recopied these letters all yesterday evening. I cannot erase that last sentence, "We must manage to survive," from my mind. A letter from July 1939. Thirty-eight years, almost to the day, have gone by since then, and the same anxiety is still ever-present: "We must manage to survive . . ."

The mock dogfights of combat planes continue without a halt high above Jerusalem. Daily, routine exercises. I no longer even hear the noise of the engines. Two sonic booms, one after the other: planes crossing the sound barrier; all the windowpanes tremble and a crow perched on the wall of the garden flies off awkwardly and lands on the roof opposite. The regular hum of airplane engines begins again . . .

When was it that my father became, in his own way, a Zionist? I can't say. Doubtless when he reached a total impasse. "I would rather wage war on the Arabs . . ." Could he have predicted that his grandchildren's generation would still be at war — and their children, too, perhaps?

A few days after the end of the Yom Kippur War, I attended Avi's funeral. I had met him two years before, when he became my assistant. He was not brilliant in the usual sense of the word; nor were Shaul and the twelve others who were students in the same history seminar during the year 1973. There is something of the peasant about these sabras, something ponderous and something new.

We were reading texts of German youth movements during the twenties: the Bünde, so shrouded in ambiguity. We discussed the special new place of youth in European society of this era. We recognized the similarities between the German Wandervögel and this or that tendency of Zionism, of the left in particular — a resemblance that may come as a surprise. We also studied in detail the avatars of our homegrown nationalist right, which at the beginning of the thirties also preached a cult of youth, on the model of Italian fascism; these Birionim of Abba Achimeir's were not very important groups, but their movement was copied from the most fanatic of those to be found in Europe in the same period.

Avi was going to write a paper on the Bünde, while Shaul had chosen Achimeir and his group. Both of them were planning to present their work to me in the autumn, so as to begin their doctoral studies immediately afterward. They were called up in the first few hours of the war. On October 13, Avi sent me a card:

Sinai, October 13, '73, 1630 hours.

My dear Saul, I am taking advantage of a quiet moment to write you, on the mounting of the submachine gun on the hood of my jeep. That seems rather romantic, doesn't it? The reality is actually quite banal. We're still simply waiting, as usual. From time to time they lob a shell at us and we take a few shots back. And we wait.

Do you remember the group I tried to organize to discuss the Israeli-Arab conflict? We formulated all sorts of theories and were all more or less agreed that the present government was incapable of facing up to the problem. Now, more than ever, I think we must try to resolve the conflict by taking the long term into account (the national aspirations on both sides, the type of power to be established, and so on), but I'm sure there's no possible solution until we've hit the Arabs hard, until they're convinced that they can't wipe us out. I hope you're all well.

Till soon,

Avi.

Shaul, who was in command of a tank battalion, was killed on the fourth day of the war, and Avi was fatally burned in his jeep, two days before the cease-fire, in the region of Bitter Lake.

There were very few of us gathered round Avi's grave, in the rain and icy wind that sometimes sweep the hills of Jerusalem. He had suffered horribly for two weeks — bloated and disfigured, a rotting body dying a lingering death.

The wind carried away the few words that I delivered. And after all, what was there to say? The rain could not hide the new rows of graves: like Avi, many of these dead were barely twenty years old. From one war to another, are we about to cover the hills of Jerusalem with newly carved gravestones?

July 6, 1977

The V.'s house faces the walls. When we left them, the full moon made the battlements look unreal. We stopped spontaneously in the doorway, without a word. A silent, instantaneous communication.

> *He calleth to me out of Seir:*
> *Watchman, what of the night?*
> *Watchman, what of the night?*
> *The watchman said,*
> *The morning cometh, and also the night:*
> *If ye will enquire, enquire ye:*
> *Return, come.*

My father abandoned the electrician's course, and in the hope of obtaining a Canadian visa left for Aurillac to learn a trade that there was a great demand for on the other side of the Atlantic: cheesemaking. My mother continued her training as a beautician, and I was placed in a "home" for Jewish children, near Paris, at Montmorency.

One of these children was named Jacob. He spent hours at a time sitting on his bed, absorbed in a pile of illustrated magazines.

He had very white skin, green eyes, a black yarmulke on his head, and brown earlocks on each side of his face that he partially hid behind his ears.

It is difficult for me to say today whether all the children there were pious, but many of them were, among them Jacob — to my misfortune. He noticed immediately that his prayers were as foreign to me as his Yiddish, his yarmulke, and his earlocks, and alerted the others. I was a non-Jew, a *goy*. And so the little Jews of Montmorency were to avenge themselves for all the things that the *goyim* had made them suffer — whether they had directly experienced them or not — them, their families, and the entire Jewish people. I was on my way to becoming doubly Jewish.

I was tied to a tree and beaten. So many nightmares rush in and gather round this instant! I can still see the tree and, if you can believe me, I can still remember the bark and feel its greenish roughness, and see, farther away, the spacious building where we were lodged, surrounded by a long terrace. A sunny day, flower beds, mown lawns. Beaten by Jewish children because they thought I was different from them. So I belonged nowhere. At that moment the only thing I knew was that my parents were far away and that the children terrified me. I screamed in terror and knocked my head against the tree trunk.

My cries alerted the women in charge of us. One of them took me on her lap. I was trembling so violently that for a long time I couldn't get a single coherent word out. I finally calmed down, but the harm had been done: I was a three-year-old child again, and every morning I was sopping wet with urine when I woke up. I was transferred to the "baby" section: everything there smelled bad, but at least they didn't bully *goyim*.

I remained at Montmorency a good six months longer. It was

a period of continual suffering, not because of the bullying, which ceased, but because of the separation from my parents.

Weekdays were bearable, for I lived in anticipation of Sundays and in the hope of a visit. At the beginning of my stay in the home, both my parents came to see me, but when my father left Paris, my mother was unable to be with me every Sunday. And I never knew in advance which Sundays she could come.

Was there a telephone at Montmorency? I was never called to one, and every Sunday morning the same anxious wait began. From the terrace circling the building one could see, where the trees did not block the view of the street, the approach to the main gate, for a distance of about a hundred yards. As soon as breakfast was over, I would go up on the terrace and begin my watch. From time to time a visitor would arrive for another child, and this made me even more downcast. I could stay like that for hours, abandoning my post only to eat and then going back to it immediately afterward. Sometimes afternoon found me still there, though I knew by then that my mother would not be coming.

Most Sundays, however, my mother did come. Till lunchtime every moment was happiness to me, but after lunch the fear of her leaving came over me. However vague they may be, my memories of those days are centered on one precise spot: the arbor.

On leaving the "home" and walking down the street, we arrived at a café surrounded by a garden. In this garden was a grape arbor and under it two or three tables. There, in the afternoon, before leaving again, my mother would often come and sit with me. And so all the sadness that a child is capable of feeling is concentrated for me on a perfectly ordinary scene: on a summer afternoon, a little boy seven years old sits across from his mother under the arbor of a café in Montmorency. In front of them are two glasses of lemonade, but they are not empty, despite the heat. In about an hour the mother will leave. Nothing more than that.

This period is only incidentally reflected in a letter written at the time by my father: "Our little boy doesn't like it very well in the institution we have put him in, and this — as you can imagine — troubles us a great deal . . ."

3

"The possibility of continuing on is a chapter in itself," my mother wrote to her friend in London on August 23, 1939, the day after the pact between Nazi Germany and Soviet Russia was signed.

In the present situation, one can hardly count on Palestine. My brothers go on doing all they can, but we are very skeptical. Moreover, it's almost funny to worry our heads about it. But can we count on you English? Perhaps there won't be a war after all. We will doubtless know more tomorrow. In any case, how did you feel about it yesterday?

In the Métro early yesterday morning. I was reading the headlines in other people's newspapers as usual and I almost fainted: last night I listened to all the radio stations I could get, beginning with Germany (did you hear it?). Even though you felt more or less like crying, you had to laugh nonetheless, despite the fact that everything was less and less clear. All we can do now is wait as calmly as possible and let everything take its course. In the meantime I have signed up as a nurse for the Czech colony. If only we were not constantly tortured by the thought of those who have not been able to get away. My mother has just received her visa for Sweden, but will she still manage to get out? In actual fact, I don't think they'll do anything to old people, I just can't believe it . . .

. . . For the moment, if there is any future for us here, I hope to be able to use my newly acquired knowledge. I am already working a little, and if I had any faith in all the promises I've been made for the fall, I'd rent a five-room apartment immediately. But since we've just had a collective lesson in modesty, I'll be quite satisfied if I can manage to feed us.

Perhaps Hans will find work, too. I've been very lucky: I'm attending language courses where I meet people who have all secured work permits thanks to their contacts, in this case with the Czech consulate. I've also managed to get one and perhaps Hans will get his card very soon (???). He's already received a notice to appear at the prefecture . . .

The letter continues the next day: "Today, now that they've made the text of the pact public, there's no sense in worrying one's head about anything. The only thing left for us to do is not to think too much about our own fate; something much greater is at stake now. Will we survive? I am very calm and hope for only one thing: that we will be able to hold out as long as possible. Perhaps we'll see each other again . . ."

Eight days later, the German armies entered Poland and the war began. I was transferred to another "home," a more attractive one than Montmorency. What was more, I was beginning to get used to things.

War bulletins put out by the French High Command were read to us in the dining room. As I asked for an extra helping of mashed potatoes, I learned that "our forces" had entered the Sarre basin and taken prisoners. More than once we admired the convoys of light tanks on their way to the front and the training maneuvers of the Moranes above the airport at Toussus-le-Noble. The debacle followed. For me it was a pleasant memory.

Huddled up next to my mother, I made the journey from Paris to Néris-les-Bains in the Allier, crammed into a train compartment with a dozen other people. My father was to join us the next day. Just before entering the station at Orléans in the middle of the night, we were surprised by German planes, and the flares and bomb bursts caused immense confusion. I snuggled up still closer to my mother and, amid the cries and the general tumult, I remember chortling with pleasure.

The two years we spent in Néris left me with the impression of being a happy period. It is easy to understand why. All three of us were together again, and better still, we were crowded together in the intimacy of a tiny dwelling.

"Néris-les-Bains," the Petit Larousse says, "commune of Allier, arrondissement of Montluçon: 4,600 inhabitants (2,650 within the city limits). Mineral waters." Clearly, the Larousse doesn't tell everything. If I had to choose a definition, I would venture to affirm that Néris was Vichy on a smaller scale, which is not very precise, or perhaps, in the period that I am speaking of, it was Vichy on a smaller scale minus the government plus the Jews.

The waters of Néris were well known before the war for their beneficial effects on nervous people, a fact that now became perfectly ironic. Hotels, family boardinghouses, and apartments for rent abounded, in a peaceful setting of avenues shaded by chestnut trees. With the defeat and the exodus, all of them filled up with a host of people taking a cure against their will, some of whom had been habitués of the spot. Almost all of them, as I have noted, were Jewish.

Thinking back on it today, I tell myself there was some dreadful irony surrounding the choice of this city as a refuge, from the very fact that it was a little town for vacations and relaxation, characteristics that Néris tried to maintain as though nothing had happened. In the morning the "sick people" left in groups to take their cure; during the day those who could afford it installed themselves on the terraces of the cafés or ambled slowly along the tree-lined avenues in the parks; when night fell, people went to the casino to hear the orchestra play the latest popular songs — songs from Paris.

There were two categories of those "taking the cure": those who lived in the "center" of the town and those who, like us, found ourselves on the periphery. When you enter Néris from Montluçon, the road divides in two: the main fork climbs the hill, runs past the city hall — a neoclassic-style building, as I remember — and then the square in front of the church and the school, whereupon it leaves town in the direction of Commentry; the other fork heads off to the right, becomes the main avenue of the park and passes in front of the hotels, runs along the casino and its gardens, and then, past the spa, heads upward again, becoming simply the rue de la Poste and rejoining the road to Commentry. It goes without saying that people who were well-off lived in the vicinity of the right fork, while the rest stayed near the road leading out of town.

Among the Jews, one could make out two quite distinct groups from the beginning: the French and the foreigners. Even their common plight did not entirely erase this dividing line. Aronson and Fauchon belonged in one category; Friedländer, Meltzer, and Fraenkel in another.

As for the "real French," in Néris, as everywhere else, only a small fraction of the population divided into two opposed camps.

On the one side were the three schoolmasters, fiercely anti-German and anti-Pétain from the very first, as well as a number of "patrician" families of the city, the M. de L.'s and the T.'s, in whom we were soon to find our most faithful benefactors. On the other side were members of the "*grande bourgeoisie*," also half provincial and half Parisian, about whose Pétainist — and anti-Semitic — feelings there was no doubt.

All this was evident only later, for during the two years of our stay in Néris no one, as I have already intimated, seems to have been prevented from "taking the waters," from sometimes listening to the orchestra on the terrace of the casino, from seeing *Troika in the Snow* or *Stagecoach* at the movies, and, as far as the children were concerned, from receiving postcards signed by the Marshal's own hand . . .

When we arrived in Néris, my mother was thirty-five and my father forty-three. To summon up the picture of my mother during this period, I have only to choose at random among the many memories I have of her, which from this time on are very clear ones. I am sitting on the bed, the door opens, and she comes into the room: her thin, straight silhouette stands out against the light behind her. A radiant smile brightens her face; most noticeable of all is the gay look in the huge brown eyes. Her chestnut hair is slightly wavy and worn very short, in a tomboy cut almost, which accentuates her ordinarily energetic, decisive manner. Her clothes also contribute to her air of a woman who is still young and active: nothing filmy, drooping, iridescent, but rather, simple tailored suits, plain ones even, and — the curious preciseness of memory — shoes with flat heels.

Slightly taller than my mother, my father looked much more frail. In Néris he was already very ill. His unusual air of distinction apparently struck everyone who met him. There was something intriguing about his facial expression — child that I was at the time, it even impressed me: it came from the apparent contradiction between his generally distant and severe air and the marked gentleness of his gaze and features. But then didn't this contradiction rule his entire existence? On the one hand there was his penchant for music, books, meditation, and on the other the particularly arid and rigorous legal and financial career he had pursued. Thus my mother's energy and vivacity stood in strong contrast to my father's reserved, contemplative, and more and more melancholy attitude.

As I write today, I have already reached the age my father was when he disappeared, I am already older than my parents were in Néris. I contemplate them from a distance, from very far off, and I ask myself: What blindness led them from mistake to mistake to the very end? What dark destiny? I endeavor to understand, to put myself in their place, to imagine what I would have done, but I am unable to . . . Even today, I look at them only through the eyes of a child.

I remember a quarrel the two of them had. They were in the kitchen. My mother had turned quite pale and made a gesture with her hand as though to hit my father; he raised his arm, too, more or less as though to protect himself, and gave a sarcastic, bitter little laugh. When they saw that I was watching, the quarrel ended immediately.

Quite naturally, my mother became our principal financial support. From this time on, she was to accept any and every task and any and every humiliation. It began with making the rounds of the farmhouses in the area and the interminable discussions with the peasants: "But, monsieur, last week a liter of milk cost only . . ." We fell back on goat's milk instead and in place of potatoes were content with Jerusalem artichokes. And then, as the beautician she now was, my mother gave massages and removed her customers' unwanted hair countless times. When one of them came to our house, I would sometimes follow the operation from one corner of the room: a swollen, hairy leg was bared, my mother covered it with brownish wax and then suddenly tore off this ephemeral plaster, strips of which piled up in a basin, bristling with hundreds of hairs. I am quite sure this precious wax was later melted down over the gas burner, strained, ridden of the hairs of the ladies of Néris, and then used all over again. Most of the time, it was my mother who "went to the customer," carrying an enormous satchel, like the Jewish peddler of the fairly recent past become a reality once again. But the little money she earned came largely from the housework she did; it was by going out with her sometimes, especially on Thursdays when there was no school, that I caught incomprehensible but memorable glimpses of a provincial Catholic bourgeoisie that I later came to know far better.

The long childhood illnesses I had were happy times for me. In those days chicken pox or measles cases were still strictly quarantined, and my mother was obliged to stay with me longer than on ordinary days. We chatted together and I read her a few selections from my first literary work, "The Serpent of the Pampas."

In the meantime, my father's health got worse and worse. The stomach ulcer that even in Prague had made him suffer now tortured him daily. In his case there was no diet possible, no medicine that worked, no operation that could be performed. I can still see him, lying stretched out on the bed for hours at a time, his face drawn, trying to rise above the pain as best he could: "I, the undersigned, Dr. Georges Bon, former intern of the hospitals of Paris, physician at the hospital of Montluçon, certify that I have treated Monsieur Hans Friedländer, a refugee residing in Néris-les-Bains.

This patient is suffering from a duodenal ulcer, with frequent periods of intense pain, and his general state is deplorable. The patient is unable to do any sort of work. Montluçon, June 19, 1941."

What is more, his apprenticeship as a cheesemaker had been futile. He finally connived to give a few lessons — in German. Fate had chosen a fierce irony.

At times my father became good humor and gaiety personified, above all when the best of our friends and the most beloved of men, Fraenkel, an obese, jovial Viennese Jew suffering from heart disease and asthma, puffed up our three flights of stairs, opened the door panting, collapsed on the first chair in sight, and burst out without even catching his breath: "Have you heard the latest one? The police arrest a Jew in Marseilles; he doesn't know a word of French, nothing but Yiddish. 'Are you Jewish?' He realizes what's up and shakes his head violently. 'Well then, a Catholic perhaps?' The answer is still no. 'You're pulling our leg: a Protestant?' Still no. 'What nerve — don't tell us you're Greek Orthodox.' The Jew's face lights up, he gestures joyously, and cries '*Ot, ot, ot*'" (which means "That's right, that's right" in Yiddish).

Tell another, Fraenkel!

"The war is over. A Jew is back in Vienna again, reading a newspaper in his usual café. A man comes over, sits down beside him, and after a moment asks him, 'Could you lend me that paper when you've finished reading it?' It is Adolf Hitler in person, in civilian clothes, very polite, shy even. Then the Jew, remembering everything he's had to go through, everything his people has suffered, draws himself up fiercely and retorts, 'Lend you the newspaper, Herr Hitler? Never! . . .'"

But often my father foundered in a sort of wordless sadness. He would go sit on a bench, the same one each time, near the viaduct, and remain there a long time. Thinking back on my father sitting there, motionless in the dying light, when sometimes I ran to join him after school, I occasionally wish that he had been unable to think things through, that he had been too sick to do so. Otherwise, he could not have helped but bow to the evidence: his faith in complete assimilation had been mistaken; his failure to recognize the Nazi danger total; his confidence in France ridiculous. We should have been in Palestine or Sweden, like my uncles and my grandmother, at least out of Hitler's reach. Doubtless the worst thing of all in those days was to go on waiting, reduced to complete passivity.

What could my father have done? Nothing depended on him now. A safer hiding place depended on the goodwill of others, as did fleeing the country. Rebellion had no meaning for the few scattered Jews who saw the vise closing. Whom would they attack? The Néris gendarmes? Even stoic acceptance of misfortune was impossible. How could one resign oneself to the probable misfortunes of others, of the child who has just arrived at a run, all out of breath, announcing from a distance the great news: a good grade at school or a big harvest of dandelions?

In any event, my father was hunted down for what he had refused to remain: a Jew. What he wanted to become, a man like others, had been taken away from him, leaving him no possible recourse. He was being refused the right to live and no longer even knew what to die for. Much more than an impossibility of acting, his desperate straits had become an impossibility of being.

Like the scattered debris that floats on rivers, drifting and colliding at the mercy of currents and whirling eddies, and finally ending up piled on the shore, the foreign Jews of Néris, and the majority of the foreign Jews in France, were driven from pillar to post by contradictory instructions, false rumors, and the ever-changing constraints of everyday life: without people to help, too visible, their chances of escaping the net that was about to close in on them were meager, indeed.

For my father, the few books that he had been able to bring out of Czechoslovakia with him perhaps came to form, from time to time, a magic screen against an unbearable reality; they opened up an inner domain of calm and consolation. Their titles are still familiar to me: *The Golem*, of course, the cover of which was decorated with the "hairless face, with prominent cheekbones and slanted eyes"; a beautiful edition of *Faust* bound in blue leather; *Niels Lyhne*, the melancholy novel by the Danish writer Jens Peter Jacobsen; and the moving, mysterious *Notebooks of Malte Laurids Brigge*, by Rilke, who came, like us, from Prague.

Leafing through these volumes left to me, I have more than once pondered what profound affinities, what reminiscences, what associations could have caused my father to make this particular choice. The impossible reconstruction of a sensibility that never revealed itself to me, whose only remaining trace is my uncertain memories, these books, and a few scattered letters written in the grip of a mounting distress . . . My father would often reread, meditate: sometimes, I am sure, he saw himself back in his vanished library, with everyone gathering round about him once again.

It was usually with my mother that I made the rounds of the neighboring farms, but when my father was not in pain I would go with him to buy milk halfway between Néris and Commentry. We would walk along side by side, not saying much of anything, and sometimes my father would take my hand. Through this simple gesture he doubtless wanted to express everything; and I understood. How much closer I felt to this sick, weakened father than to the forbidding person of the Prague years! His hand held out to me and walking along in silence were all that I needed.

My friend Uri has just sent me a text in which I read these words, delivered by a young soldier of '67 during a meeting of the Ein Shemer kibbutz. "We are a generation marked by doubt and skepticism. All we have left are contradictions and a faith in ruins. What can we still believe in? I want to know. I want to know where I am going and what I am fighting for. I refuse to be an eternal Isaac mounting the altar of sacrifice without asking or understanding why . . ."

And yet our faith was monolithic in the beginning. It seemed to be able to stand up to every sort of test, to all the onslaughts of reality. We were not stupid at sixteen or seventeen, but at the same time we had the same received ideas as everyone else. At the high school in Natanya, as everywhere else. I arrived there after a few months' stay at the Ben Shemen school, of which I have already spoken, to finish my secondary studies.

It seems only yesterday. Once a week our director, the good S.L., swept into the room, enthusiastic, eloquent, sputtering, for the *Ezrahut* lesson, the lesson in civics. These classes, which might have turned into the most elementary sort of indoctrination, on the contrary opened up vast perspectives, for S.L. went far beyond the problems of our new state and tried to make us understand the great political and ideological conflicts of the time.

The Shaul Tchernikhowski High School occupied a single building in those days, at the end of the main street of Natanya. A park, Independence Park, was all that separated us from the beach. In such a setting, our thoughts might have been far removed from Lenin's *What Is to Be Done?* or the suicide of Otto Weininger, a Jew who hated Jews to such an extent that he killed himself. S.L., however, captivated us by his exuberance; for him, as for everyone else, our new state was the culmination, at once heroic and natural, of a history with no other possible ending. From this point on, everything was simple, with the exception of a few secondary problems. Everything was clear.

One has only to leaf through the albums of photographs of that time to recapture the reassuring, unquestioning mythology that was ours in those days. I have rediscovered one of these albums, sumptuously bound in beige imitation leather . . . I cannot help contemplating it with a certain incredulity. A mere twenty-five years later and everything looks to me like one immense sentimental print of the nineteenth century. I choose at random: "Grandmother and grandson on their way to the homeland": two heads, those of an old lady and an adolescent boy, leaning out of a porthole, their smiling faces turned toward an invisible shore. "The Nesher cement factory, whose products are shipped to the four corners of the world": two huge smokestacks and vast trails of white smoke that cover the sky with their triumphant spirals. "A Hasid, rescued from Russia, manufactures roof tiles": a Jew with a long beard and earlocks, his head covered, holds up a roof tile with as intense a gaze as though he were holding the Torah: prayer and work. "From Romania to an orange grove on the Plain of Sharon": a young girl, fresh as the dawn, gracefully holds up a branch of an orange tree laden with fruit; an almost voluptuous image of youth and fervor. "The blessed fields of Emek Israel": furrows stretching to the horizon. The vision of the infinite . . . "A Bulgarian fisherman in a fishing village near Elath": a miraculous catch, the vision of abundance. "An immigrant from the United States": a movie actor's face, a cigarette at the corner of his mouth, he is sitting astride a magnificent tractor, against the vast background of the sky. And finally, "Born in

Israel." It is all there; the pride in this sabra's eyes, the disciplined strength of his expression, his blond hair and blue eyes. The new man, facing a radiant destiny.

But why resort to albums? In February 1949 — I was barely sixteen at the time, it is true — I wrote to France:

I don't know what sort of a winter you've had, but I must say that here, despite the latitude, this is a very disagreeable season. It can rain in torrents, for days at a time, without stopping for a minute; and along with it comes a gale that makes it seem as though the roof of your house is about to blow away. Add to that the fact that our school is located on the seashore, and that on the coast we always have double our share of bad weather, and you can imagine the delights of spending the winter in Israel. "Ein Davar" (never mind), as people say here: you get used to everything eventually, even the climate of the country, and, what is more, building the state (and this is not an idle word here) occupies everyone's energies, and leaves us no time to think of "things beside the point."

Cultural life is not neglected here, however; on the contrary. I won't go into details, but will merely mention the brilliant musical season this year, despite the war, with Leonard Bernstein's stay of almost two months in Israel.

Under the English mandate, the Jews did their best to keep all the archaeological discoveries they were making secret, for everything got shipped off to the British Museum, but this secrecy is no longer necessary now and each day brings new treasures to our country's museums.

I think I've already bored you too much with my chitchat . . .

I was as full of admiration of my seventeen-year-old friends, those "born in Israel" (the sabras), as Tonio Kröger was of blond Hans Hansen or blonde Inge Holm — and for the same reasons (it was in these days that I first read this beautiful story by Thomas Mann). We went on outings to Galilee: brief stays in the kibbutzim of the north, where the austere beauty of a new society unfolded before our eyes; campfires and romantic sentries armed with simple billy clubs; purple sunrises above Mount Tabor; exhausting marches in the summer heat; and then, the last night, an exuberant return through the streets of Haifa, descending along the coast just in time to see the ruins of Caesarea disappear in the night, and finally, the apotheosis of the return by way of the main street of Natanya, already nearly asleep: from our three trucks fifty voices chorused at the top of their lungs some verse or other of a Russian song in its Hebrew version:

Ani ehie komissar Adom
V'at achot rahmania
(I shall be a Red commissar
and you a nurse)

or else an original Israeli song:

Moti, Moti, Moti
ʒe lo stam bahour idioti
(Moti, Moti, Moti
is not just an idiot boy)

In my last year in high school, I wrote a paper on one of the first Hebrew novels, *The Travels of Benjamin the Third* by Mendele Mokher Sforim (Mendel the Book Merchant), a watered-down imitation of *Don Quixote*, a Don Quixote from a shtetl. I have forgotten the rest of my paper, but not the last sentence: "And now Benjamin has left on other travels, ever journeying toward that horizon where, it seems to him, the earth is about to touch the sky." Israel in those days was a son of a collective Benjamin the

Third, with the same fundamental characteristic and the same excuse as he: an extraordinary naïveté.

Was there a real change in my vision of things during my three years of military service that followed? The enthusiasm of my early days in Israel began to dwindle, certainly, giving way, little by little, to a contradictory vision — without the real dilemmas of our situation being apparent to me, for all that. What lay behind this growing contradiction between a basic faith and the more and more problematical aspects of daily life?

I was becoming more and more aware of the future dilemmas, almost impossible to grasp, of this first period.

Even before I go further, there are readers who will answer that I was experiencing the most common, the most ordinary sort of disenchantment, that having to do with the imperfections of every reality as compared to the perfection of the dream, the disenchantment that always comes with an awakening, with the morrow of any revolution, the disillusionment called forth by every faith in a utopia. I grant this, and even in these early days, I think I understood it. There remains the question that has no general answer, the question addressed to everyone as an individual, which only the individual, as such, is capable of answering — for himself and not for others: what is the point, the invisible line beyond which the imperfections of everyday life come to undermine the very meaning of the undertaking?

When I finished my basic training, a heart murmur caused me to be assigned to a noncombatant unit, and I found myself behind a desk in Jaffa. Outside of my duties, which occupied me eight to ten hours a day and sometimes nights as well when I was on guard duty, I spent a good part of my free time reading. And it was through books that I became aware of how much, at the level of my sensibilities at any rate, I was a person divided. It would not have occurred to me to read a novel or a poem in Hebrew, even though my new language had become as familiar as French to me, for the little I knew of this literature gave me the feeling that I would find nothing in it. It was the other culture, the one that my own books, for the most part French ones, furnished me, which I missed as a fish beached on sand misses water, a bad metaphor, but one that seems to me quite appropriate to the situation that I am trying to describe.

It was impossible to read all the time. Quite often I spent my evenings strolling with a few friends down the streets of Jaffa. Around us were streets with Arab names, Arab houses, but the Arabs themselves were gone: the war was on. In their place were Bulgarians, Romanians, North Africans, the new Jewish immigration, the Israel of tomorrow, no doubt. The lighthouse of the port, almost abandoned, barely lighted a pitch-black sea; along the vacant lots that stretched from the port to the center of town, parallel to King George Avenue, prostitutes waited for customers; in the little cafés dice players engaged in endless games and drank glasses of arak, the anisette of the Middle East, while soldiers loitered about everywhere in idle groups, not knowing what to do with themselves. For all of us the pleasures of Tel Aviv were too expensive and raids by the military police almost something to be hoped for — they at least brought a little excitement.

On the whole, however, I didn't ask myself too many questions as yet, even when, during the long office hours, I would sometimes put aside my work, in spite of my sergeant major's stripes, take a paper covered with my scribblings out of a drawer, and finish my secret masterpiece: to go from the Étoile to Odéon, it was necessary to transfer at Châtelet . . . In short, I was reconstructing, from memory, and very imperfectly, the map of the Paris Métro, and inventing problems for the fun of solving them.

At a modest personal level, I was thus pondering the question of roots, the question of faith of an entire society. But for many, myself included, the recent past remained and still remains a massive justification.

It was in Néris that I began to be an avid reader for the first time. For my eighth birthday, my father bought me my first real book: *The Adventures of Sinbad the Sailor.* I was on my way. From that time on, I devoured everything that came to hand, from collections of children's stories and classics for adolescents, Jules Verne, Karl May, Jack London, to books that my mother sometimes borrowed from the municipal library. That was how, shortly before leaving Néris — I was not yet ten — I finished Pearl Buck's *The Patriot*, which my mother was also reading. And naturally my insatiable appetite for books took me almost every day to the library run by Madame M. de L.

Madame M. de L., who must have been already over sixty at the time, was one of my father's few pupils: it was she whom my parents were soon to turn to. A small woman with silvery hair, green eyes, and a hooked nose, she was an imposing figure. She ruled her library, her house, and everyone about her with an iron hand, but her authoritative manner could not entirely conceal a profound goodness that was all the more genuine for being hidden. I have fond memories of this old lady, who first guided my early reading and later played a decisive role in my life, to which I will return. But she was only one of the persons in Néris who did their best to give us a helping hand. I would reproach myself, for example, were I to forget our three teachers.

The school, with the courtyard and its plane trees, its playground, and the complex of buildings divided into three sections, according to the sacrosanct rules of primary education, resembled in every way, it seems to me, or nearly so, the one where le Grand Meaulnes in Alain-Fournier's novel left behind him such a powerful impression. In our school, the children all had the accent of Montluçon, a harsh one I imagined was like that of the Widow Destouches's son in his story. Monsieur Delaume, the director and the older students' teacher, always reminded me of Alain-Fournier's good Monsieur Seurel. But, unlike his young heroes, I began in the class for the youngest children and never got beyond the intermediate class in Néris.

It was Monsieur Martin who guided our destinies in the beginners' class. He breathed heroism into us. When I arrived, just before the armistice was concluded between France and Germany, Monsieur Martin had just been demobilized. Day after day he would tell us about his battles and of the derring-do of French soldiers. He got the message across to us that the German victory was merely temporary and that with just a little patience we would surely see the dawn of the day of deliverance. Monsieur Martin was very forthright in his comments, as was his colleague, Monsieur Confesson, the teacher in charge of the intermediate class. In addition to what he had to say to all of us, the latter took it upon himself to encourage me personally. He had come across, where I do not know, an old album of photographs of Prague. After class he would often invite me up next to him onto the platform at the front of the classroom, and, while two kids swept the room, as in *Le Grand Meaulnes*, and the dust flew up around us and it began to get dark, he would turn the pages of the album and comment: the Hradčany, the Malá Strana, the statue of Jan Hus. "What a beautiful city!" he would exclaim with an emotion I shall never forget. "You'll see it again, you can be sure of that!" As for Pascal Delaume, he was soon to play his role in my story.

Meanwhile, the days went peacefully by, punctuated by trivial incidents that when I think of them now seem to me to convey a world of meanings by the mere fact that they are associated in my mind. For instance, I was invariably at the top of my class. One day, when I came home and proudly announced some recent triumph, my mother said to me, "Come, come, it's not that clever to be best of the children in Néris!" I was mortified by this remark, as the fact that I still remember it proves, but I accepted it as being a fair one.

As I have already said, I sometimes accompanied my mother on Thursday afternoons when she went out to do housework somewhere. One day at the S.'s, my mother was polishing the living-room floor. I was sitting in a corner. The entire family had gone out, except for the two daughters of the household, who had just come back from boarding school in the region. From behind the curtains there suddenly came the sound of whispering and laughter and then the words "Dirty kikes, dirty kikes . . . ," whereupon the two little girls shrieked with laughter till they were breathless. My mother blushed, hesitated for a moment, and then continued polishing the floor without a word. One still had to make a living.

I have mentioned gathering dandelions. In fact, we soon extended the range of what we gathered for food, from mushrooms in the forest of Commentry to wild blackberries that grew on the hedgerows in the vicinity. I swiped cherries, gathered linden blossoms, gleaned wheat and barley in the fields; I also got used to eating — like many others — rutabagas and Jerusalem artichokes. These made the new potatoes that my mother dug up from the little plot of ground we had been given behind the house all the more delicious. She had done so just in time, before someone could steal them. To heat our house we had — also like many others — a coal stove, and I imagine that I was not the only child in France who tried, in the evenings, to roast chestnuts, potatoes — and clay marbles as well — beneath the coals.

Sometimes I climbed up into the attic and hoisted myself up to the dormer window in the roof. I would stick my head out and survey the horizon: no, the Germans weren't coming. But if they had come . . . I imagined massacres, for all I would have had to do was install a machine gun, shut my eyes, and pull the trigger.

In the newsreels of the time it was the Germans who were winning. Week after week I saw the lines of Russian prisoners grow longer and the tanks with the black cross advancing. I saw Sebastopol fall, and Tobruk; the *Hood* was sunk, and the *Prince of Wales,* too. At home my parents said, "America has entered the war, it's only a question of time now." But who can know how much time each of us has left?

4

One night in December 1941 we all gathered together at the Fraenkels', in the Villa Jeanine.

Among those present were Fraenkel, his wife (an Austrian who was not Jewish), and their son, Georges, whom I called Jojo, a boy of about eight, with whom I went to school, gathered snails, and stole occasional glances at our little neighbor girl balancing back and forth on the stair railing high above our heads.

As Madame Fraenkel spread a white tablecloth on the table and laid out the silverware that had mysteriously survived every disaster between Vienna and Néris, along with the long-stemmed crystal glasses, Fraenkel told stories, as was his habit, his asthmatic pauses adding a special effect to his natural exuberance. Then he got up, opened a standing cupboard, and took out a small eight-branched candlestick, which he placed on the buffet. He lit the candle that serves to light the others and passed it to my father, who lit the first candle of the candelabrum. It was Hanukkah, the Festival of Lights.

Madame Fraenkel had prepared the traditional potato latkes, my mother had brought cabbage stuffed with a little real chopped meat, and Fraenkel poured wine diluted with a great deal of water into the crystal glasses. My father pulled out his chair, took me on his lap, and told the story of Hanukkah.

He explained to me how people had tried to force the Jews to deny their faith, and how the Maccabees had taken arms against their oppressors, broken the yoke of Antiochus Epiphanes' tyranny, and delivered Jerusalem. He also told how at the moment that they were about to relight the sacred candelabrum, they noticed that only a single amphora of oil remained, and then, miraculously, this single day's provision burned for eight days, till more consecrated oil reached the Temple.

More than one Jew suddenly discovered, like my father in his total distress, some tiny detail that brought him closer to the collective past, some childhood story doubtless long forgotten that he suddenly scrutinized with a hesitant, timid gaze.

When crises occur, one searches the depths of one's memory to discover some vestige of the past, not the past of the individual, faltering and ephemeral, but rather that of the community, which, though left behind, nonetheless represents that which is permanent and lasting.

It has been said that to be a Jew is to continue, from generation to generation, to tell a story with blurred outlines. To be a Jewish child in Néris during the war was to hear the story of Hanukkah, in deepest silence, without asking the slightest question. The usual remarks at table, the jokes that no longer hid a growing anxiety, had given way to the telling of a story that I did not understand except for the essential facts, one that, over the years, was to become fraught with questions because of the very circumstances in which I had listened to it. Perhaps the essence of a tradition, its ultimate justification, is to comfort, to bring a small measure of dreams, a brief instant of illusion, to a moment when every real avenue of escape is cut off, when there is no longer any other recourse.

In July 1942, arrests of foreign Jews in France began simultaneously in the occupied and unoccupied zones. Up till then the Germans had encountered transportation problems, following the massive requisition of rolling stock demanded by the offensive in the East. At the end of June, however, the Wehrmacht was able to free enough trains to allow a convoy of Jews to leave France every other day. The initial plan called for the deportation of a hundred thousand Jews from the occupied zone and fifty thousand from the "free" zone, but such a large-scale operation could be undertaken only with the active cooperation of the French police. The details of the negotiations between the general of the SS, Oberg, and the prime minister of the Vichy government, Pierre Laval, are well known. To try to save the French Jews, Laval demanded that the first wave of deportations include only foreign Jews, and at the same time he approved the active participation of French police forces in the planned operation; moreover, he suggested that the Germans deport children, too.

On July 16, 1942, the great roundup began in Paris. Nearly thirteen thousand foreign Jews, among them four thousand children, were herded into the Vélodrome d'Hiver. Adolf Eichmann let it be known that beginning on July 20 there would be sufficient space for children in the convoys destined to leave for the East before the end of August.

A few days later, the first convoys of deportees from the unoccupied zone crossed the line of demarcation. The Vichy authorities first handed over the five thousand foreign Jews already interned, then arrested seven thousand more during the month of August. Thrown into a panic by these rapid developments, my parents decided to hide me at any cost. But what refuge did they choose in their panic? A children's home near La Souterraine, in the Creuse — a Jewish children's home.

Pascal Delaume, the director of the public school in Néris, took it upon himself to accompany me to the institute. We took a train and then a bus, and on a splendid August morning we reached this welcoming home, surrounded by ponds full of flowering water lilies.

We left my suitcase, and Monsieur Delaume took me on a tour of the ponds while he waited for the return bus. We had both noticed the magnificent open white corollas, which lay within reach of our hands. Good Monsieur Delaume, wanting to pick one of the water lilies, advanced cautiously to the water's edge, suddenly slipped, and sank both his feet in the mud. The incident ended with no harm done and with no water lily, but I remember I noticed that our beloved director, whose smooth black hair had suddenly changed place on his round skull, was wearing a toupee.

Why am I lingering over such details? It is because Pascal Delaume, a quiet father of a family, probably close to fifty, a slightly ridiculous figure thanks to his plumpness, his toupee, and his clumsiness, has come to symbolize for me the good-hearted man in the full sense of the word: he scarcely knew us, and in any case prudence should have suggested that he do nothing. At the moment that the roundup of Jews was beginning, at a time when the police were being more zealous than usual, was there any reason for him to make this trip, risking being questioned and at the very least seriously inconvenienced? Was there any reason for him to lift a finger when people were wary of giving us so much as a friendly glance? Beloved Pascal Delaume, I never got past the intermediate class in Néris, I was never one of your students, but for me you will always remain an examplar, and a far-off friend.

Memory's strange reconstructions. The perfect clarity of a summer morning, but, at the same time, a pervasive fear. A fear with no apparent justification, but one that was there nonetheless, lurking in every corner.

To all appearances, the home was a relaxed place, on vacation. A series of sports competitions had been going on since early that morning. About a hundred children, maybe even more, boys and girls, were running, jumping, competing at swimming and ball games. On every hand there was nothing but happy cries and laughter.

For the first time since Montmorency, I found myself among Jewish children again, but this time the memory they left me with was quite different. I was immediately aware, without the slightest hesitation, of the distinctly Jewish nature of this home. There was the children's physical appearance first of all, the look in their eyes, no doubt, and their names as well: Sigi, Isi, Manek. Unusual-sounding names to me at that time in my life, and when I hear them now in everyday life they inevitably call to mind for an instant that memorable August stay at the home. But more than anything else, it was their songs.

It was about five o'clock in the afternoon, when the winners in the sports competitions had received their prizes, and we were gathered together to have an afternoon snack in the big dining room on the first floor. There were several teachers with us, and one had an accordion. When we had eaten, he began to play, and then even a child such as myself, so unlike the others, felt — quite naturally — the nostalgia, the beauty, the melancholy of those Yiddish songs, of the world they expressed, a world that, at that very moment, was disappearing forever.

Soon all the staff of the home hurried through the dining-room doors and everyone repeated in chorus the best-known refrains or verses of these songs. I, too, began to catch the melodies:

Tchiri boom, boom, boom
Tchiri boom, boom, boom . . .

The evening meal was gay, and since it had been a long day for everyone, we soon went to bed.

The fact that I had left my parents didn't make me sad that day, for I knew they were in Néris and it didn't seem like a real separation. I had no difficulty going to sleep that night.

A terrible din woke us up about two or three o'clock the next morning; in a few moments the upstairs landing outside the dormitories was filled with children in pajamas. Downstairs in the entrance hall gendarmes in helmets were bustling about. There was a sound of engines running outside; the truck drivers hadn't even taken the trouble to turn off the ignition, thinking, no doubt, that it was not going to take long, or conscious of the intimidating effect of this background noise.

Someone read out a list: those whose names were called had to get dressed immediately. Shortly thereafter, the ones who would be leaving were lined up in two rows in the hall. All the children over ten were being taken away. The next day, the gendarmes announced, they would be coming back for the others.

That evening they gathered us all together in the dining room: the big ones — I was one of them — held the little ones by the hand. My companion must have been five at most: I can't recall his name, but I remember that his nose was running, that he squinted terribly, and that despite his tender years he looked sad and resigned. One of the teachers told us we must be brave and above all march along in absolute silence. He added — something that still strikes me as mysterious — that by hiding in the forest we would be helping the Red Army in its struggle. Perhaps he was trying, for one night at least, to inspire in us the heroism of partisans, who also slept in the woods, and in this way obtain discipline and silence. At this point the door of the dining room opened; a woman entered, looked at all these youngsters about to depart, raised her hand to her face, and suddenly collapsed.

We left by twos. The march took place without mishap; I heard no sound save the crunching of pebbles and the occasional snifflings of my little comrade. We entered a forest and soon received the order to halt in the clearing where we were to spend the night.

I didn't sleep. I had no feeling of danger, quite the contrary: the warm breeze, the rustling of the trees, the wispy clouds that from time to time drifted across the stars filled me with a sense of well-being.

Did the gendarmes come back? I couldn't say, for the next day Madame Fraenkel arrived, and she and I returned to Néris.

August 2, 1977

What became of the children of La Souterraine? Thus far, I have never tried to find out.

We Jews erect walls around our most harrowing memories, and our most anxious thoughts of the future. Even a story complete to the last detail sometimes turns into an exercise in hiding things from ourselves. These necessary defenses are one of the chief features of our most profound dread.

N.G. came to visit me: she is working on a thesis on "the perception of death in Swiss and Israeli children." She shows a series of pictures to hundreds of children of the two countries and asks them to identify them, to comment on them. These two images, for instance: animals with terrified eyes are fleeing gigantic flames; and a cemetery, whose graves bear no religious markings. The Swiss child sees a mortal danger in the first picture and identifies the second as a cemetery; the Israeli child often says that the animals are playing and that the other picture shows a park . . .

I was in Jerusalem at the time of the commemoration of the twenty-fifth anniversary of the uprising in the Warsaw ghetto. That evening we listened to a radio program evoking memories of life in the ghetto. One of those who had escaped recounted the following scene: It is night. The curfew has sounded. The streets are deserted. Sitting in his room, by the light of a kerosene lamp, he stares at a piece of bread. Should he eat it then and there or keep it for the next day? Suddenly he hears a prolonged but unintelligible cry from the deserted street. He leans out the window. The cry is repeated. At first he sees nothing, then spies a silhouette painfully making its way up the street: a child. And the child cries, more and more faintly. A *shtikl broit*, a piece of bread! Soon he is directly under the narrator's window, and the latter makes up his mind: he takes the piece of bread that had been the object of his reflections and his greed, leans out the window, calls to the child, and throws him the bread. The child is lying on the pavement, and the bread falls right next to him; the child does not budge. "Reach out your hand, to the right!" The child still does not budge. "Look, lift up your head, there's bread right next to you!" The child remains motionless. The monologue goes on for a few moments until suddenly the narrator understands: the child is dead.

We were moved by this story. The next day we discussed it with a number of people. Each of them listened without comment.

"Is it possible," my wife, Hagith, says, "that, twentyfive years later, the narrator still has no notion of what he should have done? The strange thing is that none of those who heard the story here in Israel seems to have understood."

"What do you mean?"

"Don't you see, either? Instead of throwing the bread down and calling out directions through his window, the narrator should have gone downstairs, opened the door, and taken the child in his arms . . ."

A few days after my return to Néris, the last scene of our family life of which I have any memory took place. All three of us — my father, my mother, and I — were in the same room; it was night, and the room for some reason was lighted only by a bedside lamp. My mother was packing suitcases: one that I was to take with me, two or three that my parents were going to take with them; the rest, with what had followed us about since Prague, would be left with friends. This time my father was leaving his books behind (all except one — I don't remember which), as well as suits that were all familiar to me. I did not suspect at the time that after the war I was going to wear those same suits, scarcely altered. They must have given me the grotesque appearance sometimes taken on by an adolescent wearing out-of-fashion adult clothing. But it didn't matter: these abandoned suits, found by chance and worn again, became the outward sign of a continuity, that, in this case, could only seem grotesque.

My mother was carefully folding shirts and suits. The three separate and distinct piles of garments strike me today as the symbolic expression of the final, definite breakup of our family, but it is always after the fact that mute things manifest themselves as so many signs.

I remember my father saying, "Meltzer has just heard on the radio that the Germans are entering Stalingrad." My mother stopped what she was doing and sat down on the bed; I joined her. All three of us looked at the open suitcases whose well-worn leather, indestructible straps, and proud monogram "J.F." seemed like so many ironic provocations of the past.

The very day I left for La Souterraine my mother had written to Madame M. de L.:

In my despair I am turning to you, for I have learned through my husband that you have taken pity on us and understood what was happening to us.

We have succeeded, for the moment at least, in saving our boy . . . but I don't want to leave him where he is, for today one can no longer have any confidence in a Jewish institution.

I beg you, dear madame, to agree to look after our child and assure him your protection until the end of this terrible war. I don't know how he could best be safeguarded, but I have complete confidence in your goodness and your understanding.

My husband's fate and my own are now in God's hands. If He wishes us to survive, we will see the end of this awful period. If we must disappear, we will at least have the happiness of knowing that our beloved child has been saved.

The little one has plenty of clothes, underwear, and shoes, and there is also enough money for him. I will leave everything with you if you will have the great kindness to tell me yes.

We can no longer exist legally [Legal können wir nicht mehr existieren] . . .

The letter was written on two pieces of paper of different sizes, in a hand that in places was not at all clear, so my mother added at the end: "I beg you to excuse the appearance of this letter. My hands no longer obey me."

The Abbé Bonnet,* an old priest with white crew-cut hair and enormous glasses concealing almost blind eyes, came to Néris to get me. This gentle, affectionate man was taking me off to an entirely new world, to the strictest Catholicism, to an almost Royalist, ferociously pro-Pétain, anti-Semitic France, to the ladies of the Sodality, who were going to save a soul but who were also taking serious risks, because the soul they were saving was that of a Jewish child.

The extraordinary mechanism of memory: the unbearable is effaced or, rather, sinks below the surface, while the banal comes to the fore. I have only one precise memory of this initial moment, when I passed from one world to another: the ugliness of the city, the dreary look of this industrial suburb lost in the Bourbonnais called Montluçon. The weather, moreover, was fine. The sun shining on a city such as Montluçon makes a particular sadness well up. Certain contrasts arouse intense emotions; this one gave rise to a diffuse anxiety. But I am probably just combining the anxiety of the separation from my parents with my first memory of a city in reality no uglier than any other.

As I entered the portals of Saint-Béranger, the boarding school of the Sodality where I was to live from now on, I became someone else: Paul-Henri Ferland, an unequivocally Catholic name to which Marie was added at my baptism, so as to make it even more authentic, or perhaps because it was an invocation of the

---

* All the names associated with my stays in Montluçon, the Indre, and Sweden are fictitious.

protection of the Virgin, the heavenly mother safe from torment, less vulnerable than the earthly mother whom at this very moment the whirlwind was already sweeping away.

An adult conversion may be a purely pro forma affair, and there were many such during the war, or it may be the result of a spiritual journey that ends in a decision freely made; nothing disappears, yet everything is transformed: the new identity then changes one's former existence into a prefiguration or a preparation. The rejection of the past that was forced upon me was neither a pro forma affair — for my father had promised not only to accept my conversion but to assure me a Catholic education if life later resumed its normal course — nor, of course, the result of a spiritual journey. The first ten years of my life, the memories of my childhood, were to disappear, for there was no possible synthesis between the person I had been and the one I was to become.

My father had written the following letter to be handed over to the directress:

I am very happy to learn through Madame M. de L. that you are prepared to welcome my only son into your institution . . . and raise him in the Catholic faith.

It is with gratitude that I consent to and formally authorize you to baptize him. My wife and I promise to continue your work along the lines that you have laid down, as soon as God's will and circumstances permit us to see to his education ourselves.

I understand my father's letter: in the same circumstance, in the face of the same drama, would not I, too, have written the same lines, given the same authorization, made the same promises? I never knew whether these promises had been explicitly demanded; this is not impossible. On this point my parents were at peace with themselves, for from this moment on they accepted one goal, one essential imperative: saving their child. And in the face of so much distress, I can only tell myself: happily, not for what became of me, but happily for them, no religious allegiance stood in their way and the step was taken without doubt and guilt coming to the fore. But what, I wonder, would a religious Jew have done if confronted with such a terrible dilemma?

The day after my arrival the directress, Madame Dutour, gravely received me: "Your parents, my dear boy, have turned you over to us. You are going to have to work hard and learn your catechism quickly so that Jesus may count you one of his own. Here is a sheet of paper with the Our Father and the Hail Mary written out on it; you are to recite them to me tomorrow. Madame Chapuis will prepare you for your baptism and set the hours for your lessons. So go see her right away, and remember to learn your prayers."

During this time, my parents had been desperately seeking a hiding place. My father, whose ulcer was getting worse and worse, had just been admitted to the Montluçon hospital. In her letter to Madame M. de L. my mother had also written:

Even if my husband is allowed to remain in the hospital for a few days, I must find him a place to stay before he gets out. I, too, can remain where I am for only a little while more. I think the best thing would be a farm somewhere around Néris. Obviously, what we need are people we can rely on. Poor people would perhaps be better; we could offer them some material recompense for the services rendered. It is important to be near Néris, because I have friends there who could bring us the necessary food . . . I do not know how to thank all the

people who are helping us in this time of need. The kindness of our
friends is an immense comfort to us . . .

My mother did not find a farm somewhere around Néris. She
was allowed to stay with my father at the hospital for a few days,
but after that they both had to leave immediately. The vise was
about to close. There was only one chance left: to cross the border and flee to Switzerland. And I could not follow them on this
dangerous path; the risks were too great. Even Montluçon was
perhaps no longer safe enough for me. On September 3 my father
wrote in French to our protectress:

*I learned yesterday that the directress of the institution intends to keep
Paul here with the aim of giving him a primarily scientific education;
they would start preparing him for secondary studies now. I am grateful
to the directress for these intentions, but in view of the present circumstances it is not my ambition to make Paul a student. You will doubtless
understand that we are clinging to the hope of seeing our child grow up
in a more or less agricultural setting in which physical development is
stressed. He may not learn so much there, but he will probably find more
of the feminine tenderness he needs so badly these days. As for the certificate of primary studies, he will certainly have the chance to prepare himself for it. It was for these reasons that we were happy you chose the house
in the Indre as the place where he will live in the future, and therefore we
earnestly beseech you to urge the directress at Montluçon to transfer Paul
to the other house as soon as possible. Our poor boy has suffered a great
deal in these last few days. The beneficial effect of a peaceful countryside,
and a tranquil, tender environment, will help his child's soul to forget.*

*You can surely imagine how happy I would be to discuss this with
you and learn your opinion. But I know that you are about to leave,
and who knows what will become of us before you return . . .*

"Our poor boy has suffered a great deal in these last few days," my father wrote. That was true. If my arrival in Montluçon itself left me with only vague memories, my first days at Saint-Béranger, on the other hand, are engraved forever on my memory.

Saint-Béranger educated its pupils in a Catholicism that was particularly strict, even for the time, and did everything possible to encourage priestly vocations. The first days in this strange new setting left me with a memory of complete despair.

As I was still only a little pagan, my contacts with the other children at the beginning were extremely restricted. It was felt better to segregate me like this, out of prudence first of all, but also to shield me from the hostile attitude of some of my new comrades, especially Gilbert from Lorraine. In short, I was reliving my experience at Montmorency, but this time in the normal course of events . . .

I had almost nothing to do except learn my catechism lessons, and as I did not yet have a place assigned me in study hall, I spent a good part of the day in the parlor, a little reception room that was almost always empty. I stood for hours at the windowpane, looking out at the terrace, bordered with a few plants, and the dusty courtyard down below. One afternoon it rained: I found it a distraction or, rather, a relief.

In Néris, I used to like installing myself in the little shed alongside the house where the bicycles were kept, and watching the rain. One afternoon my mother, returning home from some job or another, had come and joined me. We had sat down on a big Dunlop automobile tire that happened to be there, which doubtless came from the factory at Montluçon, and the two of us watched the gray curtain of rain and listened to the raindrops' gentle splash. My mother had put her sack with a few provisions down beside her, but in her hand she held a soaking-wet leaf of a plane tree, a leaf that autumn had already turned red and gold; she gave it to me to dry and put in a book.

In Montluçon the weather cleared after a few hours.

Everything at Saint-Béranger stifled me: the austere discipline, the continual prayers, of which I didn't understand a word, the dreariness of our dark building, and, finally, the food, which seemed revolting to me. I don't know why, but I imagined that the rubbery meat that was served us on the day after my arrival was cat meat.

The "cat meat" and the general upset in my life had a pitiable effect on me, adding a grotesque touch to the overall picture that only accentuated my misery: on my second night at Saint-Béranger I was gripped by a severe diarrhea and had to get up out of bed a good twenty times, as I remember. The next day everyone was put on a diet, for it seemed impossible that one child could have caused that much commotion. I forthwith acquired a dubious notoriety.

But what was happening to me was experienced through the filter of a single thought, a single desire, a single drive of my entire ten-year-old being: I had to rejoin my parents at any cost. It was more than distress or nostalgia, it was a physical need, so to speak, and nothing could stand in its way. While I had left for La Souterraine without feeling sad, I felt, with the inexplicable instinct of children, that if I couldn't manage to rejoin my father and mother before they left the hospital at Montluçon, this separation could be final.

I decided to run away.

Madame Chapuis taught me catechism at the caretaker's lodge, occupied by her brother. Hence I was able to inspect at my leisure the little front courtyard of Saint-Béranger and the gate that led to the street, but I was terrified by the personality of the brother, a Cerberus who was both lame and one-eyed. I was convinced that this disabled man, who in reality was the gentlest and most harmless of creatures, had guessed my plans and would lay a trap for me at the last moment. I would wake up at night with a start, pursued by this Cyclops's limping footsteps; during the lessons, the apostolic Roman Catholic Church disappeared in a fog the moment the caretaker's blind eye was turned in my direction.

Despite my terror, on the first Sunday of my stay at Saint-Béranger, at the beginning of the afternoon, when everything was quieter than usual, I went and sat down on the bench in the front courtyard, as unobtrusively as possible, waiting for Chapuis to leave his lodge. He went out around three o'clock. I ran to the gate, opened it a crack, and found myself outside.

I had succeeded in making my escape, but where was the hospital where my parents were? A ten-year-old child finds his way by asking people. The passersby whom I questioned may have been astonished to see such a little boy running about all alone like that, looking for the hospital. But could anything really have surprised them at that time?

At the hospital information window, I asked the way to my parents' room. I was told which one it was. Even today I am unable to understand why my parents were hiding there under their own name: can their assumed name have totally disappeared from my memory? But how would I have known it?

I climbed up four flights of stairs, opened the door, and threw myself into my mother's arms.

There are certain memories that cannot be shared, so great is the gap between the meaning they have for us and what others might see in them. Undoubtedly the words exchanged in this hospital room were, objectively, simple, everyday ones: the pleas of a child and the promises of adults.

I was sitting on my mother's lap, with my arms around her neck, weeping. Everything was white in this room, the enameled whiteness of hospitals. There were several beds in the room, but they were empty just then. The room opened out onto a balcony that ran the length of the building and allowed one to go from one room to another. That was how my father came in to join us.

The red splashes of pots of geraniums fastened to the edges of the balustrades contrasted with the overall whiteness. We had had geraniums on the windowsill in Néris, too; it was my mother and I who took care of them. We watered them carefully and cautiously. When winter came, we had to make sure the frost didn't kill them, but what joy the moment the first flower opened in spring!

On this hospital balcony were chaise longues and a little table, also painted white, on which there was nothing but letter paper, an inkwell, and a fountain pen: no balls of yarn or knitting needles. In Néris, however, my mother used to knit in the evening. She had made me a pullover, a scarf, and mittens, for — have I already mentioned this? — it was freezing cold in Néris in winter and all the children got chilblains. Since the end of the war, curiously enough, chilblains seem to have disappeared. I don't know how my mother had managed to come by the wool, but, in any event, the pullover she knit for me — and that I took to Montluçon — was white, with horizontal red stripes; the mittens also had colored stripes. My mother wanted everything to look pretty.

My father was paler than usual that day; he was unshaven and kept pacing back and forth. Though the weather was nice, he was wearing his woolen sweater for around the house, a light brown one with a thin blue stripe along the neck edge. A doctor came in and went out on the balcony with my father. I saw my father shake his head; the doctor left and my father came back into the room.

There was a continuous hum of voices in the corridor and along the balcony, too, outside the neighboring rooms: visiting hour. From time to time a burst of laughter. The light was already changing.

My father and mother spoke in turn. They assured me end-lessly that we would not be separated long. Meanwhile, it was abso-lutely necessary that I return to Saint-Béranger. No, I wouldn't be going with them: they couldn't tell me why, but it was better that way. I would soon be joining them. What was more, the war would be over shortly and we would go back to Prague; then everyone could . . . — and here my mother used a rather vulgar Czech expres-sion to lend the conversation a gay note, to show me that there was no reason, really absolutely no reason, for me to be unhappy.

I was quite aware, however, that there was anxiety in these words: my parents were pleading with all the conviction of those who know that they are not going to be believed. And at that point something happened that was a sign.

A phone call had been made to Saint-Béranger. Madame Chapuis and Madame Robert arrived soon afterward, if I remem-ber rightly. I had to leave. My mother put her arms around me, but it was my father who unwittingly revealed to me the real meaning of our separation: he hugged me to him and kissed me. It was the first time that that timid father of mine had ever kissed me. Noth-ing was definite yet; others had risked taking their children with them. My parents had put me in a safe place, but here I was, a run-away who had gone straight back to them, unable to bear being separated. Could I be dragged away from them a second time? I clung to the bars of the bed. How did my parents ever find the courage to make me loosen my hold, without bursting into sobs in front of me?

It has all been swept away by catastrophe, and the passage of time. What my father and mother felt at that moment disappeared with them; what I felt has been lost forever, and of this heartbreak there remains only a vignette in my memory, the image of a child walking back down the rue de la Garde, in the opposite direction from the one taken shortly before, in a peaceful autumn light, between two nuns dressed in black.

My parents left Montluçon a few days later. At Lyons they joined a group that was gathering to cross the Swiss border. They tried their luck in the region of Saint-Gingolph. The Swiss police turned them back and handed them over to the French.

On September 30, the day they were arrested, my parents were able to send a letter to Madame M. de L. from Saint-Gingolph: "We reached Switzerland after a very tiring journey and were turned back. We were misinformed..."

We were misinformed.

A few months ago I went to Saint-Gingolph for the first time. I saw immediately that it was not there that my parents had tried to cross the border, but rather that that was where they had been taken afterward. Looking at the map, it seemed to me that the most likely place for them to have tried to cross the border would have been the little village of Novel, eight kilometers from Saint-Gingolph, in the mountains. I went there. An inhabitant of the village confirmed my guess; in the autumn of 1942, groups of Jews had tried to cross the border above Novel. Moreover, at the Hôtel du Grammont there was a dossier and a detailed account.

I went to the hotel; the owner gave me the dossier. I went out on the terrace. Not a cloud in the sky; forests all around me; to the right, the crags of Le Grammont; opposite, a few hundred yards away, the valley of the Morge: the border! I opened the dossier: "Novel — Memories, Reminiscences (1973)." And on the following page: "A nightmare stay. From September 27 to October 6,

1942." The story of a witness, Madame Francken, who lived in Novel at the time. My parents' letter was dated September 30. Madame Francken had seen things and told of them, taking ten pages to do so. Her story ended with these lines:

We never found out what became of those two! [The two in question were Czech Jews, a brother and sister.] The notorious Sergeant Arretaz of Saint-Gingolph turned people back like a sadist, whereas his confrere, the customs officer, ran and hid so as not to see the agonizing cortege of those sent back to the border, straight into the hands of the French militia. Two of these poor wretched creatures slit their wrists on the bridge on the same day, while a woman (whom we had seen being hunted down in l'Haut de Morge) threw herself from the fourth story of the hotel in Saint-Gingolph where she was staying . . .

In the course of her story, Madame Francken had written: "Switzerland lets in the old, the sick, the families with children. The others are sent back across the border and into the hands of soldiers!"

If I had accompanied my parents, would we all have gotten across the border?

Here is my parents' September 30 letter in its entirety:

We reached Switzerland after a very tiring journey and were turned back. We were misinformed. We are now awaiting our transfer to the camp at Rivesaltes, where our fate will be decided in the way that is already quite familiar to you. There are no words to describe our unhappiness and our despair. Moreover, we don't have our baggage. Can you imagine our physical and mental state? . . . Perhaps if you could intervene at Vichy we would be spared the worst. It is not the camp that we are afraid of. You know that. If there is the slightest possibility of helping us, do not hesitate, we beg you. Act quickly. There must be a solution at Vichy that would be less catastrophic for us. Don't forget the little one!

Then on October 3 a telegram was sent from the camp at Rivesaltes: "Without intervention Minister Interior, our imminent departure inevitable. Regards, Jan Friedländer, 3548 Rivesaltes, block K."

And finally, on October 5, one last letter was thrown from the train of deportees to Quakers who waited in the stations as the convoys passed through. The first lines are written in ink, then an almost empty pen had endeavored to trace lines that were subsequently gone over in pencil:

Madame, I am writing you this in the train that is taking us to Germany. At the last moment, I sent you, through a representative of the Quakers, 6,000 francs, a charm bracelet, and through a lady a folder with stamps in it. Keep all of this for the little one, and accept, for the last time, our infinite thanks and our warmest wishes for you and your whole family. Don't abandon the little one! May God repay you and bless you and your whole family.

Elli and Jan Friedländer.

What God was meant?

Part II

2

My progress in catechism was satisfactory, and at the beginning of October I was baptized in the Church of Notre-Dame in Montluçon. My first communion soon followed, as well as my departure for Montneuf, the house in the Indre that my father had mentioned in his letter.

So, sometime in the month of October 1942, I passed through the great stone arch that led to the inner courtyard of my new refuge: beechnuts and chestnuts lay strewn along the paths all around.

I could not say what Montneuf had been before becoming a boarding school — a convent perhaps. But when I arrived, the building looked more like a big farm to me than a convent: everything about it was suited to rural living. As I think back on it today, I can't help remembering with a certain nostalgia the massive gray buildings, set about the vast, irregularly paved courtyard, with the fountain in the center. And yet it was at Montneuf that I was more or less to touch the very bottom.

I was not a country child, and I felt more lost among the little peasants of Montneuf than among the young city dwellers of

Montluçon. I would have liked to wander along the ponds, pick a flower, or gather chestnuts, but instead of that I was obliged to spade the garden, to rake, to carpenter, and soon was to have to herd the cows — which frightened me more than all the rest. As Mademoiselle Cécile — whose father, she told us, was a fireman in Montauban who spent hours polishing his helmet — put it: "Paul-Henri, you're all thumbs!" My future was not at all a brilliant one, according to her. This good young woman from the South of France with her strong accent and her trace of a mustache had no way of knowing how justified her pessimistic prognoses were.

"Paul-Henri." I couldn't get used to my new name. At home I had been called Pavel, or rather Pavlíček, the usual Czech diminutive, or else Gagl, not to mention a whole string of affectionate nicknames. Then from Paris to Néris I had become Paul, which for a child was something quite different. As Paul I didn't feel like Pavlíček any more, but Paul-Henri was worse still: I had crossed a line and was now on the other side. Paul could have been Czech and Jewish; Paul-Henri could be nothing but French and resolutely Catholic, and I was not yet naturally so. What was more, that was not the last of the name changes: I subsequently became Shaul on disembarking in Israel, and then Saul, a compromise between the Saül that French requires and the Paul that I had been. In short, it is impossible to know which name I am, and that in the final analysis seems to me sufficient expression of a real and profound confusion.

I no longer remember whether I arrived at Montneuf just before or just after my tenth birthday, but it was at Montneuf that I received, through Madame M. de L., a letter that my parents had sent me for my birthday. They must have left this letter with my "godmother" before their departure from Montluçon; I don't know what has happened to it, but I remember it bore no sign of the place that it had been sent from, or of the place where my parents were at the time. They assured me that they were in good health and that I would soon be with them again; they also said everything that parents can say to their child for his tenth birthday — almost a man now, isn't that right? I was quite aware that there was something strained about this letter. Where were my parents? Were they afraid I might try to run away again? But I didn't have the strength to repeat that. In fact, I was at the end of my rope.

I began to sleepwalk. To avoid being humiliated, I decided to tie myself to the rails of my bed in the evening. I made complicated knots around my left wrist, and even though the arrangement interfered with my sleep it did keep me where I belonged. But in the morning a new problem presented itself. We were supposed to get ready for mass at a run, or almost. You can imagine the surprise of our dormitory mistress, Mademoiselle Madeleine, I think it was, when she found that instead of washing his face like the others, poor Paul-Henri was struggling to untie himself from his bed . . . I had the choice between sleepwalking at night and being late to mass in the morning. I don't know what I did then, but as for all the rest, a serious crisis was soon to change the course of things entirely.

September 11, 1977

It is absolutely imperative to distinguish between the ephemeral and the essential: the ephemeral leaves its painful marks, the essential still remains. Until the day when the ephemeral has eaten away so much of the essential that the nucleus itself is destroyed.

Examples of the ephemeral, at once trivial and extreme: the newspapers these last three days speak only of swindlers, and of a continuous colonization, overt or covert, but in any case without respite, of what we call Judea and Samaria. But does the war that everyone is talking of again, in whispers, stem from the ephemeral as well? Will we ever leave confusion and contradictions behind? Let me try here to keep to the essential, to the unobtrusive signs of the essential.

R. maintains that our entire vision of the world, all our rites, all the products of our imagination are steeped in guilt: the catastrophe of destruction and exile, brought down on the heads of a people imbued at the time with messianic fervor, could not help but arouse the image of a deserved punishment, a crushing tribute exacted as the consequence of some obscure infidelity. The return to Eretz Israel would thus be one last effort to reject this age-old shadow, a genuine defiance of our fate: we are no longer guilty, because here we are in our homeland once again, together once more on the soil of our ancestors. At any rate, that is how R. sees things.

September 13, 1977

This is the morning of Rosh Hashanah, our New Year. The streets of the city are very quiet in the sun: no cars, or almost none. Little groups hasten to the synagogues: in the peaceful light I can hear the chants of the faithful. In a few moments the long calls of the shofar, the ram's horn, will ring out. "They are long," my daughter Michal explains to me, "so that their sound will reach the seventh heaven and our prayers will be heard there..." Rosh Hashanah, 1977: thirty-five years later, almost to the day.

At mass, there were several of us who had the same difficulties. At the beginning everything went well, but after about twenty minutes, as a combined result of empty stomachs and incense, and the successive changes from a kneeling position to a standing one, one or the other of us would suddenly get up, leave the pew, walk down the center aisle of the chapel in the direction of the exit, and faint halfway there.

The victims were taken to the office of Madame Chancel, the directress, and when we came to, helped by ammonia or a renewal of strength quite natural at our age, we would often see her gaunt face leaning over us.

Madame Chancel's kindness ought to have been a source of comfort to me, but nothing seemed to be able to bring me out of the melancholic apathy into which I was sinking, little by little. I did not react at all, for instance, even when a faintly comic episode occurred in this context that to me was not at all comic.

One day I saw a boy of about fifteen arrive at Montneuf: Davy, a boy I had known in Néris. If there is such a thing as a Jewish face, his was one, there was no doubt of that, but his name had become much more French than mine even, a name with an aristocratic *de* in it. He turned up as an Eagle Scout, decked out in a magnificent uniform. He knew all about the most recent patriotic ceremonies, and soon began organizing the salute to the colors, campfires where he recited poems to the glory of Marshal Pétain, and walks punctuated with the most uplifting songs of the day; in short, Davy gave himself over to a feverish program of national revival. He passed through our midst like a hurricane, and during the few weeks that he stayed at Montneuf he never gave a sign of recognizing me: he made not the slightest effort to be pals with me. I for my part restricted myself to following his lead in a daze: I, too, gave no sign that I had met him before.

It took me several months to go under entirely. One aspect of my new existence, it is true, gave me a pleasure that no doubt compensated for other things: our walks.

I very soon came to love nature: I was capable, as much as a child can be, of feeling the communion that for an adult may become the source of the most intense joys. Even as early as my days in Néris, I had loved to lose myself in the fields or the forests round about, doubtless to live adventures, like the ones in my books, but also because I enjoyed hedgerows decked with snow, banks of clouds the color of lead, the smell of wet leaves. I also liked, I confess, something else that will probably seem ridiculous: crows — birds that in general no one likes and are thought to be ugly. I liked seeing them flapping clumsily along above the fields.

At Montneuf the rugged Berry countryside was exactly to my liking: there was no lack of hedgerows and fields, clouds, dead leaves — and crows as well. I have often wondered since why I was attracted to this sort of landscape when others, more beautiful according to classic canons, left me indifferent. What can I say about the landscapes of Israel? They are certainly beautiful, with all the beauty of the Middle East, and more impressive — that I readily concede — than the countryside of the French Berry or the Bourbonnais. And yet . . . these are affinities that go back, I imagine, to the landscapes of my early childhood.

So it is that I remember an afternoon in November or December. We were walking on the edge of a wood, the sort of wood where everything grows together in a tangle, brambles, ferns, trees; the last were almost bare and the whole formed a gray mass bristling with countless twigs. Opposite us, on the other side of the path, were fields the dark brown color of the soil, and, farther away, bordered by reeds, a pond reflecting the sky. The sky itself, covered with huge stretches of dark clouds, was transformed, just above our heads, into a band of intense color. This melancholy landscape was beautiful to me — to the point that I felt a thrill of pleasure. But despite these fleeting joys, I became sadder and sadder: in one way or another, I was going to let myself die.

Toward the end of winter, in March, the occasion to do so presented itself. I had felt feverish for several days, but I was determined not to say a word about it. Mademoiselle Madeleine, who supervised our walks, was sometimes surprised at the apathetic air of poor Paul-Henri, but did not pursue the matter. And so we started out, as usual, on one of our outings. And as usual I loitered along a bit to the rear, all alone, for I hadn't been able to make friends with any of the children at Montneuf. The paths were real quagmires, and on the slopes the snow was still piled high in brownish drifts. I could barely lift my galoshes, my throat hurt worse and worse, and I seemed to be seeing everything through a sort of veil: I was burning with fever.

We walked alongside a brook. I fell even farther behind the group, which disappeared around a bend in the path. Without hesitating, I waded into the ice-cold water up to my knees; I knew exactly what I was doing, even though the fever dulled my senses. Suddenly Mademoiselle Madeleine appeared quite near me; I heard her questions, but her scolding seemed to me to be of no importance. Then came calls of "Paul-Henri! Paul-Henri!" on every hand, but I couldn't have cared less about the cries, the laughter, the mocking looks of my schoolmates, who had retraced their steps.

I have no idea how the walk ended, for after I had been fished out of the brook I felt sick, and from that moment on my memories are confused, blending together into a single long stretch of being ill. I was in bed for several weeks; a very bad case of croup; according to Madame Chancel, I nearly died. They didn't dare take me to the hospital, since in a little town like Le Blanc, or even a fair-sized city such as Châteauroux, a child who did not look at all like the others might have aroused suspicion. Madame Chancel installed herself near me, behind a screen, and a long bedside watch began.

How strange it seems to me today to call to mind this far-off breaking point! Was this sick child really me? I imagine that if there were such a thing as a collective Jew, he might well ask himself the same question: am I the same today as the Jew of thirty-five years ago? Yes, it is indeed me; it is indeed us. But there are deep clefts, despite appearances: everything has changed and yet nothing has.

I retain a paradoxical memory of my illness: the reality of the daily care given me, the injections, the doctor's visits, Madame Chancel's attentiveness — these have almost disappeared, whereas the scenes conjured up in my delirium are still as plain as day to me, though it's true that the most insistent of those fantasies was merely the barely retouched reminiscence of an episode that had occurred barely four years before, the episode of the train.

When our train left Strasbourg Station, I wanted to celebrate our freedom to move about again by taking a little walk in the corridor. But the corridor led to another car; a vestibule was soon stepped across; in a few moments I was completely lost. I didn't realize it immediately, for I met three boys, a little older than I was, doubtless French children who were also leaving Czechoslovakia — three boys who visited the first real humiliation of my life on me. The biggest one called to me in Czech, and after a few words asked me if I could see the Eiffel Tower. I looked out the window; no, I couldn't see it. "But take a good look, over there, on the horizon . . ." The horizon was simply that of Lorraine, but I was soon convinced; as my companions, greatly amused, gave war whoops to greet the Eiffel Tower, I went them one better and whooped in ecstasy at spying the celebrated silhouette. The three little demons galloped off, leaving me there, frightfully disconcerted and hurt, as much as a child of seven can be. I began to cry and it was then that I realized, on looking around toward the compartments to see where my mother was, that I was lost.

Panic, real panic, overcame me. I began to run from one car to the other, doubtless in the wrong direction. I made my way along, swaying from side to side with the motion of the train; I gripped the sliding doors of the compartments, feverishly pulled them open, and poked my head inside: the same tired faces in each one, the same piles of suitcases. People barely looked my way and, without so much as a question, plunged their scowling faces back in a book, in a newspaper, in sleep. My delirium made the corridors endless and the faces became threatening: I screamed in terror and, if only because of the croup, felt that I was suffocating to death. But suddenly, by a miracle, I was saved: my mother, who had set out in search of me, appeared. I ran to her, threw myself in her arms sobbing, felt the coolness of her fingers on my face . . . I opened my eyes: it was Madame Chancel stroking my forehead to calm me.

September 17, 1977

It took me a long, long time to find the way back to my own past. I could not banish the memory of events themselves, but if I tried to speak of them or pick up a pen to describe them, I immediately found myself in the grip of a strange paralysis. When I finished my military service, since I could not forget the facts, I made up my mind to view everything with indifference: every sort of resonance within me was stifled.

The years went by. I completed my studies, in stages. At the same time, various functions linked with Israel, either abroad or in the country itself, familiarized me with the concrete, day-to-day problems of our state, but I never felt the old, early enthusiasm. This activity took me even further away from a childhood that appeared to be buried once and for all, and from the world that had gone under with it.

But sometimes one awaits something without knowing it, and suddenly the slightest sign, the slightest summons, takes on an unexpected dimension. In this period this was the effect on me of a stay in Sweden at my Uncle Hans's. He was the director of an institution for children who were mentally ill, at Tulsa in the Swedish countryside, south of Stockholm. At the end of 1956 I came simply to pay him a visit; I stayed with him a year.

We almost never spoke of Prague or Rochlitz: sometimes memories follow their own indirect, mysterious paths.

As far as its outward appearance was concerned, Tulsa bore a certain resemblance to Montneuf: the same very low buildings around a central courtyard, the same stretches of fields and forest all around. It was in this setting, which had a certain charm, that I learned to know children who lived amid delirium, in the inaccessible world of their fantasies, those who wanted to speak and could not, those who desperately sought to establish human contact and would merely repeat a name, for hours, or else sing the same song, punctuated with tosses of their heads, over and over again. I realized then what was meant by an inner world closed off forever . . .

At Tulsa I also discovered certain books in my uncle's library. It was made up largely of works on anthroposophy, but among editions of *The Philosophy of Freedom* and *Knowledge of the Higher Worlds* there were also three volumes by Martin Buber. That is how I came to read *On Judaism, Tales of the Hasidim,* and *The Legend of the Baal-Shem.*

I have no idea today whether I was influenced at this time by the intellectual message of these thin volumes, but I remember having been profoundly moved. I read and reread them several times, and as the result of being in a foreign country, and of a certain solitude too, I felt, as never before, the hidden grace of this secret world of Hasidism. But, more than this, for the first time I began to feel a clear difference between my identification with Israel, which for a time at least seemed to me to be superficial and almost empty of meaning, and a feeling of my Jewishness, certain aspects of which appeared to me in this unusual setting to be suddenly endowed with a new, mysterious, powerful, magnificent dimension.

June came and I was to leave soon. We were in that period of "white nights" when the hours pass slowly by in a milky half-light that chases sleep away, despite the heavy black curtains, and that favors long conversations interrupted by long silences.

In the course of the preceding weeks, I had become friends with two Germans who were doing the same work I was at Tulsa: one of them, Dieter, was very young still, born on the eve of the war; and the other, Wolf, was a man of around forty who had seen action at the front.

One evening Dieter and I were invited to dinner at Wolf's, no doubt to celebrate my departure. The meal was a gay one, and thanks to the wine and the aquavit, the Scandinavian liquor that rips your throat out, each of us talked more than usual of the present, the future, and the past as well. Wolf called up his memories of the war: he had served on the Russian front. Certain scenes came to his mind: villages burned as his unit passed by, while songs could be heard far off in the distance. Half nostalgic, half tortured, Wolf told us that he had served in a unit of the Waffen SS. I was impelled to leave the room. Two days later I left Tulsa.

When I remember this year outside of time, the evening with Wolf seems to me like a brief, violent blow, a warning and an urgent summons to turn toward this chapter of history, for nothing could be forgotten yet, and in fact nothing was over. The reading of Buber, on the other hand, was a thing of gentle, quiet vibrations, like a progressive discovery: beyond the Jewish folklore glimpsed from Ben Shemen and Natanyah, far from Biblical austerity and the cold rigor of the Law, I felt in these pages a warm, enveloping pulsation that strangely contrasted with the superficial, the banal, the transitory aspects of Israeli life in those days. There remains my encounter with the closed world of the children at Tulsa, with the powerlessness that for me became, confusedly at first and then clearly, an obsessive symbol — on a personal level, I was going to say, an actual provocation. I shall speak only of Arne and Bert, very briefly.

On a winter morning about three months after my arrival at Tulsa, I took Arne, a boy of fifteen, for his usual walk. The first snows had already fallen, but the roads had been cleared and I hoped to reach Elsgård, an institution similar to Tulsa, where we could have a hot cup of herb tea before starting back. Arne was very sick: he would pour out an incomprehensible flood of words and gesticulate endlessly as he told himself stories whose meaning only he could understand. As usual, he walked quite a distance ahead of me on the way back and disappeared round a bend at the entrance to a village, waving his arms furiously, deep in the mysterious world of his fantasies. When I again caught sight of him at the end of this village street, he had a gang of youngsters, who had just come out of school, at his heels, mimicking his screams and gestures. Panic seized Arne, who started off at a run, with the youngsters behind him, and me still farther behind, trying to catch up with them. We left the village and ran through the pristine white fields. After a few hundred yards, tired out and in tears, Arne threw himself down in the snow; forming a big semicircle around him, the children continued to shout gibberish at him, waving their schoolbags and their caps. Arne's fury then turned against himself. When I finally caught up with him, he was rolling in the snow, the whites of his eyes showing, foaming at the mouth, trying to tear his clothes off. I could only hold him by the shoulders as best I could and try to calm him by talking. A few moments later the youngsters scattered, hurling a few parting insults at him. At that point Arne suddenly gripped one of my hands and raised his face to me. Everything that was locked inside Arne's head, everything that he was never to express, all his howling, dumb suffering was there on the contorted face covered with tears, mucus, slaver, and melted snow. Arne blinked his eyes, trying to tell me everything, but how could he do it? "Herr Friedländer," he burst out, "Herr Friedländer!" — and could say no more.

As for Bert, he was a boy of thirteen or fourteen who would repeat only one meaningless phrase, "*Svalla ble*," over and over. As a matter of fact, he didn't say it, he sang it, very softly at first, and then louder and louder; soon it was triumphant "*Svalla ble*"s, always to the same tune. To calm him, all one had to do was say "*Tist*," which means "Be quiet." Bert would thereupon lower his eyes, stop for barely one second, and then start over again: "*Svalla ble*," night and day, endlessly. I am quite sure Bert never slept.

But Bert knew how to read. When you showed him a page and pointed to a line with your finger, he would stop singing his refrain, and like a machine, with no intonation, he would read the words in a rush. I decided to take advantage of this to try to reach him. We read, every night. But as soon as my hand left the page, as soon as my finger no longer pointed to the line, the flood would dry up, and inevitably his unbearable "*Svalla ble*" would start again.

One evening when the other children in the dormitory were already asleep, we installed ourselves, as usual, in the entry hall. You had to take him by the hand to get him to sit down on the bench; otherwise, he remained motionless, either standing or sitting, according to the circumstances, but unfailingly chanting "*Svalla ble.*"

We began to read, and as usual I tried to kindle for a moment a fleeting spark of communication. All of a sudden, I raise my hand, my fingers leave the page; Bert stops reading and looks at me. I wait for the "*Svalla ble,*" but Bert says nothing. He is still looking, his lips move, he is about to say something, a vague smile hovers on his lips. Still nothing. The smile persists. Is it possible that . . . ? No. His eyes grow dull again, his face assumes its fixed expression, its total vacuity, once more; his lips open, and hesitantly though distinctly the "*Svalla ble*" pours out . . .

When the *Gripsholm* slowly pulled away from the Göteborg docks, I knew that this strange stay in Sweden had opened doors for me that would never close again.

At the end of three or four weeks of illness, my breathing was normal again and my fever began to go down. I was getting well.

I watched the life of Montneuf through the window of the infirmary that looked out on the big courtyard. I could see the carriage, hitched to two horses, circle the fountain; I could follow the clumping of wooden shoes on the stones and the shifting sunlight on the wall of the building opposite; I could hear the children come out of mass, and could even make out the voice of Jean, a boy I liked. In short, in this month of April 1943, I was coming alive again. Even good Madame Chancel was surprised at how quickly I was recovering.

Spring had come by the time I was allowed to go outdoors. In the beginning I had difficulty walking, but soon I could stroll along the edge of the ponds again. The path was bordered with hawthorn in flower, and clumps of jonquils formed golden patches in the grass. I felt fine; I had changed. The memory of my parents seemed further away somehow.

During Holy Week I went back to my usual place in the chapel, without feeling faint this time, and began to assist at mass. More than once I was obliged to confess to "impure thoughts," but I became more pious than ever in order to turn over a new leaf. I was ripe for Saint-Béranger. In September I returned to Montluçon.

2

Once again it was Madame Dutour who welcomed me. She was exactly the opposite of Madame Chancel in appearance: whereas the latter was tall, pale, and frail, with a black mantilla that gave you a glimpse of two smooth wings of flaxen hair, Madame Dutour was small, dark, and Latin-looking, and had a Southern accent. When I arrived at Saint-Béranger, her hair, doubtless once very black, had already turned silver, and formed an agreeable contrast with her dark matte complexion and her brown eyes. Like the entire Sodality, both these women lived in a universe that was strange, to say the least.

In the eyes of outsiders it was a circumscribed, stifling world, but to a new boarding student eleven years old it meant calm, certainty, roots. The perspectives of this monolithic Catholicism had long since been thoroughly explored, and had no yawning abysses: they had the perfect coherence that marks any total belief. One could not be mistaken about the nature of Good and Evil at Montluçon, and I imagine that for most students — those who were not suddenly assailed by fits of indefinable terror — this world seemed completely reassuring.

In my memories, Saint-Béranger is frozen within the framework — a dusty, faded one, with a slightly rancid odor — of a whole way of provincial life, one that modernity and the Republic had spared, and one that quivered with excitement when the Vichy government was established. For Marshal Pétain was venerated in the Sodality; his effigy, like the crucifix and the image of the Virgin, inevitably adorned each one of our classrooms, the parlor, and the dining room. Shortly after my return to Montluçon, Philippe Henriot, the new Vichy minister of propaganda, began his radio campaign. We read his harangues every day; when he was executed by the Resistance, his death seemed an abominable murder to us.

When I try to picture the world of the Sodality again, it is its unreality, its sudden remoteness that seems most striking. Nothing remains, it seems to me, of what appeared immutable a scant thirty years ago. I have the impression that the Saint-Béranger of those days has suddenly been reduced to a fine dust and blown away, like a house slowly eaten away by termites. But who knows, perhaps I am the one who has become totally different, perhaps I am the one who now preserves, in the very depths of myself, certain disparate, incompatible fragments of existence, cut off from all reality, with no continuity whatsoever, like those shards of steel that survivors of great battles sometimes carry about inside their bodies.

I adapted, and became a devoted Saint-Béranger student. I was placed in the fifth grade. Like many of my schoolmates, I soon felt a vocation: I wanted to become a priest.

At that time Saint-Béranger was made up of about forty children and youths, two or three young seminarians, a few nuns — the mainstay of the school — and lay sisters. The use of our time was fixed, down to the minute, from morning prayers to those at bedtime. Chapel services alternated with classes, meals, and recesses, the whole unfolding within a tiny, fairly run-down setting, but one that nonetheless had its charms for us. The two main buildings adjoined each other, and an annex led on one side to the little front court where I had made my first appearance and on the other to a playground surrounded by a fence, and beds of Japanese privet that gave off a heady, nauseating odor when in flower. Beyond that lay the city: in the foreground a dreary square, a boulevard, and two enormous cylindrical gas tanks; farther in the distance, almost at the horizon, the military barracks and the buildings of the Dunlop factories that a bombing by British planes had recently partially destroyed.

Study halls and offices occupied the ground floor and the second story of each of the main buildings; above were the dormitories. The dining room was in the annex. As for the chapel, it was reached by a winding staircase that then led to the dormitories. We went from the dormitory to the chapel, from the chapel to the dining room, from the dining room to study hall, from study hall to the chapel, walking one behind the other, in order of size — little ones in front, big ones behind — arms crossed and eyes lowered, either silently or reciting a prayer. In the evening when we went to chapel after study hall, the damp walls of the stairway echoed with the Salve Regina, while our shadows flickered as they wound up along the walls, to the rhythm of swaying hand-held kerosene lamps that feebly lighted our way up the stairs.

The rites before sleep followed. We knelt at the foot of the bed for one last prayer, then got undressed according to firmly established rules: you took your shirt off first, so as to put on a long nightdress, harsh and faded from many washings. Then you had to open the bed by drawing down the covers and the top sheet, sit down on the bed, pull the sheet and the covers over your knees, and then and only then take off your trousers, avoiding, through this double precaution, any offense to modesty. Madame Robert walked about among the beds, checking to make sure that each of us would fall asleep flat on our backs, hands crossed over our hearts. The light would go out, a blue night lamp now the only illumination in the room. Our dormitory mistress then went into her room, a small one adjoining the dormitory, from which she could peek at us through a little window. Soon her light went out, too, and darkness enveloped twenty or thirty boys already breathing in unison.

The pupils at Saint-Béranger came from all over. Names with an aristocratic *de* mingled with the most common surnames. Children from the surrounding region lived alongside others from Lorraine, Brittany, the Midi, and even from the overseas French colonies; the three D. brothers, for instance, had come straight from Rabat, Morocco. Most of the pupils came from extremely pious families that had often produced a priest or a nun already.

There was nothing about Montluçon that recalled the sometimes cynical, often quite equivocal atmosphere that one associates with large religious establishments, Jesuit schools in particular. Of course, there were few of us, and we were closely watched, day and night. Nonetheless, veritable explosions, sudden, brief, and powerful, occasionally shook our little community. They took the form of quarrels about nothing that broke out without warning between some of the older pupils, usually during evening study hall. Astonishing in themselves in a place such as ours, those fist-fights linger in my memory because of their extraordinary violence: in a few moments noses were bleeding, smocks torn, eyes swollen, handfuls of hair torn out; the antagonists used anything that came to hand as weapons, even classroom chairs, and it often took all the authority of Madame Dutour in person to separate them. What could not be expressed otherwise found a spectacular outlet in those fights.

Our studies were based on permanent competition. Each week, on Monday morning, Madame Dutour would solemnly read the list of averages, and each class had its members in first and last place. The names of those first in each subject were posted on the honor roll, and mine was soon on it regularly. I was in the limelight: undoubtedly I was going to become a Jesuit, or rather a *jèʒe*, as the slang expression of our day had it.

At Saint-Béranger I discovered adolescent friendship. In Prague, shortly before we left, I had had a first pal, Jiří, a boy my age, also Jewish, the one who had the puppet theater where the *vodník* moved about in a greenish cavern. During our walks in Hradčany Park, we worked out plans for an impenetrable underground shelter where our two families could live in perfect self-sufficiency: we had doubtless guessed that danger was close at hand, without knowing why. These plans were futile, of course, as we know.

Later, in Néris, Fraenkel's son Jojo became a good playmate of mine, but no more than that. At Saint-Béranger, on the other hand, Paul and Georges were real friends, the sort who add a measure of dreaming to the grayness of memory. They were both from the South of France, the first from Aix and the second from Toulon. Thanks to them, since they could leave on vacations and were familiar with the wider world, I, too, participated in life "outside." I learned to be as familiar with Mont Sainte-Victoire as though I had seen it with my own eyes, and I could imagine what the sea was like before ever seeing it.

Two years ago I made an effort to see Georges again. We had occasionally exchanged letters and I knew that he had been in a monastery in central France for twenty years. Why this sudden desire to find a friend whom I hadn't seen in thirty years? No doubt the same imperious resurgence of the past that has contributed, at least in part, to the writing of this book, the same surfacing of the obscure questions of my adolescence, now returned and influencing my day-to-day outlook. A need for synthesis, for a thoroughgoing coherence that no longer excludes anything.

I found Georges, that former brother of mine, just as he had been, save for a potbelly . . . Reverend Father, how many memories come back to me! I made poor Georges talk for hours about himself, about what had happened to him during those years, and about Montluçon as well. But strangely enough I have forgotten the precise details he furnished me, or rather they are now mingled with deeper, earlier memories, forming an indivisible whole. My image of the past is like a plot of land thirsting for water. The moment a drop falls, it disappears; the moment a torrent begins to flow, it is absorbed. Even so, names did come back: those of the three B. brothers — who are not to be confused with the D. brothers — and the de P.'s also. In each of these three families, one of the brothers became a priest, thus demonstrating the hold exerted not only by tradition but by the institution as well. Not everyone escaped the influence of these highly formative years.

Did Georges understand at the time, before I told him, that I was Jewish? No, he had known nothing about it. What did he imagine, then? For him I was a Czech refugee, or something like that, a boy with vague origins. This was a stroke of luck for me, I realize today, for an indiscretion on the part of one of my schoolmates might have been fatal. As a matter of fact, they had been looking for me in Néris.

In 1944, the Vichy militia had turned up at the home of the C.'s, our landlords. "Where's the little boy?" The C.'s, in all good faith, said that they had no idea. Then it was Madame M. de L.'s turn to be interrogated: "The parents have been arrested, but where is the child?" Madame M. de L. claimed she knew nothing, and then immediately counterattacked: Weren't they ashamed? What a dirty job! What odious behavior for Frenchmen! The militiamen left without bothering her further. A good deal more than one child's life had been at stake: Madame M. de L. was Jewish by birth herself.

The first day, Georges took me across the immense fields of the abbey, to the outer walls, with their Raven Tower. Later, standing at the back of the chapel, I attended one of the services. Was there anything left of the emotion that I had once felt? No, nothing. At that level, there was nothing left.

On Sunday morning, before high mass, we went to spend a little while on the banks of the Loire, no more than ten minutes away by car. It was already hot when we set out, the silent heat of early summer. We went down toward the riverbank. The water was flowing along without an eddy, without a splash. Close by, a rock and some bushes gave a little shade. Georges talked about music, but to tell the truth, I was scarcely listening, enveloped as I was by the calm of this morning. Woods covered the opposite bank, descending to within two or three yards of the water; alongside us, gnats danced in the light and dragonflies flitted past. Then suddenly a little girl emerged from the woods, by way of a path I couldn't see from where we were sitting; she was preceded by a dog, and wore a white hat, like the ones in photographs of long ago. The dog began to run and the little girl chased after him along the riverbank; suddenly both of them came to a halt; the little girl reached down toward the dog, petted him, and talked to him. She straightened up and made a broad gesture with her hand. Everything was motionless. Suddenly the two of them began to run again and disappeared in the woods. Georges was still talking.

Did he see the little girl and her dog, too? "Alban Berg, to be sure . . . ," he was saying.

September 20, 1977

The conversation with Claude is hard to forget. He told me about his film. The last sequence finished was with a former SS officer at Treblinka. The man refused to be identified, but he finally did agree to talk, in a hotel in Braunau am Inn, Hitler's Austrian birthplace, near the German border. When he entered the room with his wife, this SS officer was confronted with a huge map of Treblinka covering one whole wall: he lost his self-confidence, he wept, he sang Nazi songs, he sang the Treblinka song. He told about his troubles with a certain Sturmbannführer Wirth: Jewish women were running stark naked along the labyrinth of fences leading to the gas chambers; they were defecating in terror: should their excrement be removed? The SS officer gave the order that this be done; Colonel Wirth refused. The controversy arouses, excites the SS officer once again as he tells it. "But tell us, sir, from the point of view of organization, wasn't it difficult to kill eighteen thousand people a day without leaving too many traces?"

The heads of the women of Treblinka were shaved just as they were about to enter the gas chambers. The shaving was done by ten Jewish barbers at once. Claude has located one of them: he is still a barber, in New York. He tells what it was like at Treblinka. And the notorious Perry Broad of Auschwitz tells his story in the film, too, as does Murmelstein, old Murmelstein, whom we still consider to be a traitor, the chief of the Jewish council of Theresienstadt; he, too, tells his story, beneath a soft spring sky, in Rome.

A mad wind turns the pages of the past. There are some unknown ones here: the children of Bialystok, for example. In

1943, two hundred Jewish children, from Bialystok in White Russia, are transferred to the Theresienstadt camp in Slovakia: an unusual movement, from east to west, from centers of rapid extermination to a more merciful transit camp. When on the first day they are taken to the showers, an immense outcry is heard: "Gas!" They already know, but this time all they are gathered together for is showers. For two months the children remain there in Theresienstadt, cut off from the rest of the camp. Then they disappear forever. Who are they? Those children were to have been sold to Jewish aid organizations, the first step of a bargain whose proportions might have been tremendous. But the negotiation fell through: the children were killed.

"Tell me, sir," Claude asks the officer from Treblinka, "which burned faster, men's bodies or women's?" The SS officer calmly begins to expatiate.

Long walks were one of our real pleasures. We would leave early in the morning, right after mass, on foot, for a destination at least ten kilometers from Montluçon. In the city itself, we would walk two by two, little ones in front, big ones behind, as usual, and I imagine that with our berets and capes we must sometimes have been a strange sight. We would meet German soldiers who were also walking two by two. The most astonishing posters covered the walls and the fences, and I can still remember the image of a snail glued to the very bottom of the Italian boot, with the American and British flags on its horns and the inscription, in English: "It's a long way to Rome."

Sometimes we walked past the hospital, and I would feel my heart miss a beat, a passing anxiety. When we circled the building, I would look at the rooms on the fifth floor, wondering if one of the glass doors wouldn't suddenly open and my mother or father lean out over the edge of the terrace to signal discreetly to me. But would they even have recognized me with my hair cut in a pageboy, my gawky legs, my socks that drooped over worn shoes, my beret pulled down over my ears, and my midnight-blue cloak?

Once we had gotten past the town's slag heaps, we were in the midst of nature, delighted to be attacking forests of pine and beech, running through the heather, scaling rocky hills to station ourselves at the foot of some ruin, splashing about in brooks. It is difficult to describe the mad joie de vivre that came over us on such occasions. Everything that could not be expressed in any other way came out in the course of these outings, these chases, these games of cops and robbers, of cowboys and Indians; in short, we were normal, happy children. When night fell, we would fall in line spontaneously and march home, singing "Marshal, here we are," or "Nothing is impossible to a valiant heart."

In my own case, these explosions of gaiety were only intermittent, like so many sudden reactions of an organism subject to a tension triggered by little things. How can I forget, for instance, the mail calls?

When Madame Robert appeared each week at the top of the terrace steps with her arms full of letters, everyone crowded around — myself included. Ought I to have kept apart from the rest when the names began to be called? How could I explain that I knew in advance not to expect anything, that this time, too, there would be nothing for me? I waited, from one week to the next, for three years. And the strange thing was that, as the presence of my parents began to become blurred in my mind, their letter, the one that never arrived, became more and more important, more and more laden with nostalgia and vain expectations. Dare I say it? I have the impression that, as time passed, the letter corresponded to a more immediate need than my parents' return; this symbol of love and attachment took the place of the persons themselves.

Because I received no letters or visits, and because I never went on vacation, my schoolmates realized that I was different. In their eyes, I suppose, I was already an orphan. I had only one recourse: religion. I threw myself into it with a passion.

In any case, religion dominated our lives. Mass, the adoration of the Holy Sacrament, and meditations marked the essential moments of our days, which, in addition, were punctuated by the prayers that preceded and followed meals and classes, by brief Aves murmured as we walked from one place to another, as well as by the edifying books read aloud (the lives of saints, for example) at mealtimes in the dining room. It would be wrong to imagine that we experienced this religiosity of every moment of our day as an unbearable fetter: most of us lived it with fervor. We told our beads, tried to outdo each other in ardor, were tempted by mortifications of the flesh, and, had we been allowed to wear sackcloth and a hair shirt, we would have done so with enthusiasm.

During Holy Week we learned by heart the story of the Passion according to Saint John, first in Latin and then in Greek. Which of us was not gripped with emotion on reciting the last words of Jesus to the apostles, on the evening of the Last Supper? "As the Father hath loved me, so have I loved you: continue ye in my love." The visit to various churches on Holy Thursday elated us, and the Good Friday services overwhelmed us: we were literally following in the footsteps of the Savior, imagining His sufferings, weeping at His death, exulting at the news of His resurrection.

I had passed over to Catholicism, body and soul. The fact that the misdeeds of the Jews were mentioned during Holy Week did not trouble me in the slightest. Sometimes, especially during walks, I would even relate the dark intrigues that the usurer Abraham had plotted against the noble companions of Kościuszko, exiled on the outermost borders of Siberia, embellishing, for an ever-eager audience, the adventure stories that were occasionally read to us at mealtimes.

Thus, in my own way, I had become a renegade: though conscious of my origins, I nevertheless felt at ease within a community of those who had nothing but scorn for Jews, and I incidentally helped stir up this scorn. I had the feeling, never put into words but nonetheless present in me, of having passed over to the compact, invincible majority, of no longer belonging to the camp of the persecuted, but, potentially at least, to that of the persecutors.

Each of us has certain secret shames, those brief instants buried in forgetfulness that provoke an immediate burning sensation when an association brings them back to conscious awareness, an instinctive disgust, immediately followed by the desire to see those memories blotted out forever. For me it is the stories I told of the usurer Abraham and his intrigues.

And yet, when Madame Robert, who taught philosophy to those rare pupils at Saint-Béranger who entered the last form, sang the praises of Bergson, I was secretly proud of learning that so great a philosopher could also be Jewish. Bergson was born a Jew but later came very close to embracing Catholicism, though he refused baptism. Madame Robert even suggested that God would surely count him among His own.

The simple unquestioning faith drummed into us was, as I have said, the one I needed. Wasn't this literal Christianity addressed first of all to the disinherited and forsaken of this world? Had God not tested me because he loved me more than the others, thus pointing out to me the road to sanctity? All these thoughts elated me. But my greatest comfort was devotion to the Virgin. At

Saint-Béranger the worship of Mary was the very essence of our religious universe, and in this, too, I became an exemplary pupil. Kneeling before the plaster statue with the sweet face, clad in a long white robe and a sky-blue girdle, her head crowned with tin stars, I rediscovered something of the presence of a mother.

I liked the austere simplicity, the intense devotion of the early mass at which I sometimes served, not in the little chapel of Saint-Béranger, but in the big chapel of the mother house, a few hundred yards away from the rue de la Garde. For I liked the pomp of church holidays. In reality, the big chapel had all the ugliness of plaster-saint church art, with its blue background dotted with gilded fleurs-de-lis. Yet how sumptuous it seemed to me in those days! I was intoxicated by the splendor of the chasubles and the ciboria, the heady odor of the incense, the softness or the majesty of the music; I confess that I have never again felt the emotion that used to grip me when, kneeling in the big chapel during a solemn high mass, I heard Madame Vernier strike the first chords of a fugue or even a simple hymn on the harmonium.

Paul Friedländer had disappeared; Paul-Henri Ferland was someone else.

September 22, 1977

Yom Kippur. An extraordinary silence. May I be pardoned, miscreant that I am, for continuing to write, but I must capture this silence, paint it from life, so to speak . . . Not a car, nothing. Two families meet in the street, behind the house; from the garden I hear each word distinctly: *"Gmar Hatimah Tova!"* "Which synagogue are you going to?" "Ah, you prefer the other one . . ." They have gone now. Somewhere in the distance a metal blind is raised, just enough for daylight to enter. Silence. It is nine o'clock in the morning; everything is suspended, as if by magic.

What is the link between this people and its religion? Can there be a Jewish people without a Jewish religion? As far as daily life, superficial things, are concerned, the great majority will undoubtedly answer in the affirmative, but for the essentials, I do not believe the answer can be the same . . . The alarm of a security system goes off suddenly — it is turned off, yet a dog keeps barking. Up to this moment, I hadn't heard so much as a single bark.

At the end of the day yesterday, I went to the Western Wall with my son Eli to attend the Kol Nidre service. There was no crowd at the beginning. But an hour after nightfall, people coming out of the synagogues began to descend on us in compact groups. Spotlights on the neighboring rooftops lit up the wall, and a bird, perhaps one that usually nested in one of its interstices, and frightened, doubtless, by the unusual loudness of the voices, fluttered along the wall, from time to time bumping into the enormous stones of Herod's Temple. I noticed then that when it was quite dark the cupola of the Mosque of Omar turned a dark green and that of al-Aksa became blue, a midnight blue.

The memory of another Yom Kippur, 1973; already four years have gone by since then. We were living on Metudella Street then, in a little apartment that overlooked the Valley of the Cross and the hills of the Museum. Since morning, it had seemed to me that something out of the ordinary was disturbing this day. Very early, planes flew over the city at low altitude; from time to time there was a sound of cars in the neighboring streets. Strange. At midday, however, when I was dozing in semidarkness, I had not the slightest presentiment of what was to come, despite the unusual signs that had marked that morning.

War did not seem an impossibility, it is true; there were a number of us who could envisage the eventuality of a new armed confrontation, even without a move on our part, but we expected such a war to come at some uncertain date in the future — and, what is more, we were not really afraid of it. Hadn't we all seen, with our own eyes, the impregnable blockhouses controlling the flat banks of the canal, didn't we have it on good authority that, if need be, this dirty, still water would become the most enormous seaside cemetery in history? When we called publicly for a more flexible attitude, some people called us defeatists.

Nothing could surprise me at that juncture. On the morrow of the Six-Day War, I accepted the essential points of our declared position and defended them as best I could, in spite of the repulsion I felt for the explosion of a nationalism at once simplistic and mystical. I took an active part in the contentious debates that occupied the television screens in France and elsewhere from time to time, not always without hesitation. I expressed this hesitation indirectly, in the final pages of a book that dates from this period. As the months and the years went by, and I realized that, despite appearances, our intransigence was based on principle, I openly began to stand further and further away from our official positions on various points.

No one seemed to feel any urgency in the matter. The battle between the two sides took the form of offhand arguments. The daily round of life went peacefully on and the impasse risked lasting for many years. There may have been doubts about our rights, but who could doubt our strength?

At two o'clock in the afternoon of October 6, 1973, the wail of sirens enveloped the city. "Some madman," I said to myself . . . But all of us instinctively rose to our feet and after a moment's hesitation, when the sirens didn't stop, we hurried to the stairway. On the third-floor landing we found old Judge K. and his wife, as well as Ruth H. The sirens kept wailing. Ruth, who had been listening to the BBC on this day without Israeli radio programs, passed their latest bulletin on to us: something was happening in the Middle East. I hurried back upstairs and tuned in Kol Israel on the off chance that it was broadcasting: "Syrian and Egyptian troops have attacked on both fronts. Heavy fighting . . ." That was how the earthquake began for us.

In August 1944, the F.F.I.* Resistance fighters attacked Montluçon. The city was liberated, and through the privet hedge we could see jeeps full of young men armed with submachine guns racing along the boulevard. The Germans had withdrawn to their barracks; the battle raged for a week, more or less, around the fortified rectangle. Taking turns standing on the toilet seats at night, my classmates and I could see the lights of combat; we shivered with excitement at the mortar shots — and also because we were prolonging our stay in this suspect place longer than was strictly necessary.

The Sodality did not wish for the victory of Germany, certainly, but the Resistance, which was known to be Communist and atheist, was nonetheless reviled. We were faithful to the Marshal in every way — which brings me to two incidents that have remained on my conscience. They are of the same order; the first involved Jean-Marc, and the second, little Michel.

Jean-Marc was a fair-haired youngster of about thirteen. He was very good-looking and the only one of us with artistic leanings; he had imagination and drew charming scenes, and his fingers always had huge ink stains on them. But Jean-Marc had been something of an outsider among us for some time. During a lesson in Madame Dutour's office one day, in front of a dozen of us, he began making peculiar faces. Madame Dutour paused and looked

* Forces Françaises de l'Intérieur, popularly known as "Fifis." (Translator)

at Jean-Marc without a word. Suddenly, in the general silence, Jean-Marc blurted out, "Madame, the devil is tempting me." We could smell an odor of sulfur rising.

What aggravated Jean-Marc's case were his Gaullist opinions, passed on to him by his parents. This little boy from Normandy was for the Resistance and dared to say so. Punishment was inevitable: when Madame Dutour or Madame Robert wanted to hold forth to the oldest of us about Marshal Pétain, we met in the "salon," beneath the portrait of the Savior of France. Jean-Marc was excluded from these sessions. We could see him through the glass doors, ambling along the terrace, alone and exiled, or moping about in the courtyard; to top off his humiliation, the only ones out there were the little ones, the ones who didn't understand anything. How good this made all of us feel as a group, and how happy I was to be able to share this fraternal warmth and look upon this proscribed youngster with scornful eyes! Jean-Marc left us shortly after the Liberation, whether because of the devil, de Gaulle, or his parents' decision, I don't know. But I for my part still feel the shame of having followed the others' lead.

The tale of Michel is soon told. In the course of the battle for Montluçon, we all made fun of the Fifis' inability to take the barracks. During one recess Michel, one of the "little ones," a moon-faced ten-year-old from Montluçon, couldn't stand it any longer: "But they're *French*!" he exclaimed, and burst into sobs. The others heaped sarcasm on him, and I joined in. Imagine, those no-account Fifis daring to take on the Wehrmacht!

Jean-Marc and Michel became heroes, in a modest way, by thus braving general opprobrium and giving proof of courage and independence at an age when children quite naturally follow the crowd. May they accept, thirty-four years later, this little sign of friendship and gratitude.

The barracks fell — and so did the Thousand-Year Reich. The war came to an end. I remember the day very well. The church bells pealed and the whole town celebrated. "It's not like in 1918," Madame Robert said to us regretfully. "And then there's our poor Marshal. Let us pray for him." We went for our walk despite all this, and as I remember, the general manifestation of popular joy seemed monstrous and indecent to us. Crowds were jostling each other everywhere, and people were kissing each other, obliging us to lower our eyes — without, however, causing us to make an abrupt about-face the way we had when one day on one of our walks we sighted the troop of female boarding students from Sainte-Jeanne. On the walls, crosses of Lorraine and the hammer and sickle had replaced the Allied snail pasted up by the Germans, and the whole was topped with posters showing the smug, stupid face of the imperturbable Fernandel.

There was no Te Deum to celebrate the German surrender at our school, as I remember, but instead a persistent concern for the lot of the victor of Verdun. When, later on, Pétain's trial began, we faithfully read the speeches of his defense counsel, Maître Isorni, whereas the state prosecutor, who was doubtless a Freemason, was unanimously held up to obloquy. The portraits of the Marshal remained on the walls for a long time, and when they were finally taken down, it was the end of an era at Saint-Béranger, too.

The war was over; my parents had not come back. The Red Cross thought that it had been able to identify a couple at Theresienstadt whose names corresponded to those of my father and mother, but a typhus epidemic had put the camp in quarantine, and we had to wait. An unreal wait: the days went by without a sign, and during all this time I kept asking myself: How will I greet my parents? Will there be any way to express my happiness?

A cold shiver runs up my back when I reread the letter I wrote on May 25, 1945, to Madame M. de L., who was my godmother. I was twelve and a half years old and this was what I had become:

Dear Madame,

I have a great many things to tell you. Half an hour ago I had a visit from Madame Fraenkel, and that is what I want to talk to you about:

She arrived, and after a few preliminaries, I began by asking her if she had had news of my parents. She said no and we went on to speak of my grandmother. Then this is what she said to me (more or less):

"If, let's say, your parents didn't come back, would you like to stay here?"

"I don't know. If I don't have anybody, yes, then I would."

"But wouldn't you like to go live with your grandmother?"

"Oh, yes, if she went back to Prague."

"But if she stayed in Stockholm, would you like to go live with her?"

"I don't know; I wouldn't like traveling all over."

"Why not?"

"Because it would interfere with my studies, and then . . . there's religion." (It was very stupid of me to say that, because talking about religion gets her all upset . . .)

Then she said to me:

"Religion doesn't matter. There are religions everywhere and no one would force you to give up yours."

"Why are you asking me all this?"

"To find things out! Because Madame de L. told me that you wanted to stay here. You don't want to, do you?"

"I'd rather be with my family, but there isn't anyone . . ."

"That's right! But be sure not to tell anyone what we've just talked about."

She didn't say anything else more, then . . . She began to laugh . . . And then she said to me:

"You know, I wouldn't like you to stay here either. Are you all right here?"

"Oh, yes! Just fine!"

"There's nothing you need? . . . You mustn't be afraid, you know, to tell me if there's something you need."

"Oh, if I need anything they give it to me!"

"I would have liked to have you at my house, you know."

"Oh, but that's impossible."

"I know, I almost got angry with the directress, but she wouldn't give her permission. Aren't the others allowed to leave the school?"

"Yes, for summer vacation."

"But how about Christmas and Easter vacations?"

"Oh, hardly ever."

Then we talked a little while longer. She asked me if I remembered various people and if I knew the man who was with her, waiting in the street. I said no. Then she told me that he'd known my father at the hospital (I expect she intends to stir up all her acquaintances). That is more or less everything of importance that happened. As for the rest, she promised to come back some Thursday with Jojo.

I beg you, dear Godmother, see what has to be done and talk to Madame Fraenkel if necessary. Let's hope she won't be too angry because I told you everything.

Please accept, dear Godmother, affectionate kisses from your little Paul

That year all the students at Saint-Béranger, or almost all of them, left on vacation: there were only three or four of us who stayed behind in the deserted school. We wandered idly through the classrooms, and I think even to Madame Robert the world appeared unsettled and uncertain. Our daily walks were rather halfhearted, and often we went no farther than the suburbs of the city: we trailed along the edge of the slag heaps, waiting for the sun to set on this melancholy industrial ugliness.

In the evening it was necessary to confront the empty dormitory. Madame Robert wished us good night and went into her room. A few moments later my three comrades were asleep and I was alone, staring at the vague outlines of the room by the blue light of the night lamp. Then I would begin to feel a growing, vague, intolerable fear.

Nothing is worse than a diffuse anxiety with no definite object: you feel it slowly come over you, you recognize the premonitory signs, you are terrified, yet paralyzed, before the idea of what is at hand. You can try making your mind a blank and staring at a stretch of wall, or, on the contrary, attempt to think of some precise thing (and at the time I was still quite incapable of such mental feats), but nothing helps: anxiety inexorably takes its course. Your mouth grows dry; you are either very hot or very cold, depending on the day; there is a tight feeling in your chest; your breathing becomes more rapid; your heartbeat speeds up, and sweats and chills soon follow. These are only outward signs, however, ones that you scarcely notice, remembered only after the fact, for at the moment nothing matters but the fear. But fear of what? A fear without an object, an empty fear, fear in its pure state. You are certain of only one thing: one moment more and you won't be able to stand it, you will either burst or dissolve; it is the absolute limit of what you can bear, and yet . . .

I thought that at any moment I was going to get up out of bed, scream, thrash about, run between the beds and rattle Madame

Robert's door, or else wake up my neighbor, Philippe Morin, and tell him — tell him what? I could just see the scene: I wake good old Philippe up, in the grip of total panic I shake him, he suddenly sits up in bed: "What's the matter? What's happening?" He rubs his eyes, but — it's still dark outside! Then he sees Paul-Henri, bending over him, panting. "What's the matter, Paul-Henri? Are you crazy?" "Philippe, help me, I'm afraid." But none of that happened. I didn't budge from my bed, I didn't do a thing. At the very moment when it seemed I was about to suffocate, to break in two perhaps, an ebb tide would suddenly flood over me, followed by a strange sense of well-being. Exhausted, I would fall asleep.

After a while this diffuse anxiety changed, became more precise, focused on one definite thing: from this point on, it was death I feared. But then everyone is afraid of death. I grant this, but it is still quite an unusual fear for a twelve-year-old. And, though anyone may be afraid of death, there are very few people who imagine their own death, who live through their last moment, as it were, every evening. That was what happened to me. I learned then, from experience, what "cold sweat" means, for I could literally feel an ice-cold sweat running down my forehead. I would draw my sheets up and bury myself under the covers. To no avail. Unable to divert my thoughts in any way, I would imagine the inevitable end that awaited me, whatever I did. Hiding in a dungeon, I knew that the inexorable executioner was on his way, that he would never take the wrong path or retrace his steps; one day he would open the door. I then imagined the very last instant, trying my best to cling to the very last flicker of lucidity, of awareness of being, but no, I had to slip into the void . . . One last wave bore me upward, and then the ebb tide flooded over me again.

Soon I was not safe from such anxiety attacks even during the day: like the mephitic vapors of old stories, they emerged from the nocturnal abyss to invade the twilight, or more precisely, the late afternoon, and sometimes the mornings, too.

I knew as I left on the afternoon walk that when the light began to fade, at about five o'clock, I would feel the first waves of anxiety. During all these late afternoons I managed not to say anything, not to show anything, even though my most heartfelt desire was to let other people know. But while the memory of those afternoons remains somewhat vague today, I shall never forget the fear I felt in the mornings, and one morning in particular.

I was to serve at early mass, in the big chapel. It was still dark when I arrived at Sainte-Jeanne. I put on my red cassock and was about to put on my surplice when the first signs of anxiety manifested themselves. You can imagine my panic, for this time I could not wait passively for the wave to pass. I had to serve at mass! I had to give the responses, get to my feet, make all the expected gestures, say exactly the right words — and I didn't think I was capable of doing so. I stood there motionless, my surplice in my hand, and suddenly a thought, even worse than the others, occurred to me: I was destined to live in this state until my very last moment. My life would now be one long silent torture, a continuous fear that would cling ceaselessly to my skin, that I would never be able to rid myself of. Father H. stuck his head in the door: "Come along, hurry up." I put the surplice on mechanically, picked up the censer, and mechanically started up toward the altar. I didn't stumble, I didn't drop the missal, nor the cruets, nor the ciborium, I didn't faint, and I gave the responses without making one single mistake . . . There were three of me at that moment: the one who was afraid, the one watching him, and the one serving the mass, like a machine. Was I going crazy?

I would have liked to confide in Madame Dutour, snuggle up close to her, cry my heart out, hear reassuring words, feel a caress, but I didn't dare.

And then the anxiety disappeared — for a time.

In August, Madame Fraenkel came back. She asked me once again if I was ready to leave for Sweden. I asked for news of my parents once more. Then she stared straight at me and said, very slowly and very distinctly: "My poor Paul, don't you understand that your parents are dead?"

October 4, 1977

When I leaf through these pages I often feel deeply discouraged: I will never be able to express what I want to say; these lines, often clumsy, are very far removed, I know, from my memories, and even my memories retrieve only sparse fragments of my parents' existence, of their world, of the time when I was a child. I confess that these thoughts are weighing more heavily on me than usual. Should I go on?

Outside, it is gray for the first time this season. The children will be home from school soon. For the moment everything is quiet. The usual street noises are muffled when they reach me, as though the grayness has silenced the city.

When people leave us, one after the other, their presence quite naturally anchors itself and survives in the memories of the ones who remain, in the reminiscences and everyday conversation, in the albums one sometimes takes out of the cupboard to show the children, to explain to those who never knew the ones who have departed. From time to time, flowers are put on their graves, and their names are there, engraved in stone, essential symbols, through which different generations maintain the ties between each other, follow each other, and communicate. But for me the break was an abrupt one and it cannot become a part of everyday life. What words could one use to say such things amid the happy triviality of ordinary conversations? The letters are here, and two or three yellowed photographs. For the others, these traces will soon no longer mean anything. I must write, then. Writing retraces the contours of the past with a possibly less ephemeral stroke than the others, it does at least preserve a presence, and it enables one to tell about a child who saw one world founder and another reborn.

School is out. Michal comes breezing in . . . In the oldest of the three photographs I have of my mother, she is a little girl: the same features, the same smile.

I entered the seventh grade; it was now clear that this would be my last year at Saint-Béranger. A guardianship council had taken my destiny in hand, a guardian had been appointed, and at the end of the school year I was to be handed over to his care.

Conscious of the dangers that would threaten my faith when I went back out in the world, the ladies of the Sodality, for their part, tried to forearm me against these perils. I was confirmed, and then, this time ahead of my age group, I made my solemn communion. Father L., a Jesuit and a teacher who had once been at Saint-Béranger, sometimes came to preach a retreat at Mont-luçon. He had taken a liking to me, and Madame Dutour decided that a conversation with the good father would be in order. As he was now teaching at a school in Saint-Étienne and had little free time, I set out to visit him, a little after New Year's.

From every point of view, this trip was the beginning of a great adventure for me. Just imagine: for the first time in three years I was leaving the rue de la Garde by myself: for the first time in my life I was taking the train by myself — and at three o'clock in the morning, with a change at Roanne! I must remind the reader not to forget the period: traveling by train in January or February of 1946 was an epic undertaking. In any case, for that youngster, oddly clad in navy blue, with a cardboard suitcase three-quarters empty, the threadbare overcoats, the worn jackets, and the sweaty odor of all the passengers — like the dirty snow on the slopes, the fog that let only the passing flicker of the telephone poles and the brief flash of stations through — aroused in him an intense and incomprehensible joy, a real feeling of love and brotherhood.

On arriving at Saint-Étienne, I was in no hurry to find the house of the Sodality where I was to spend the night. I strolled through the streets. I knew I was on the eve of great changes, without being able to imagine precisely what circumstances would bring them about or what they would be like. I sniffed the future.

I had received the first pocket money of my life for this trip. And suddenly, without my realizing it, I quite naturally heard all the injunctions of the past: unperceived by me, a tenuous link was being re-created. What could I have bought with these few francs in my pocket? I did not hesitate an instant, and went off to buy two books. On entering the little bookstore, I suddenly rediscovered the familiar odor of printed paper and dusty covers. These were not the splendid volumes in my father's library, but at least they were books. Not textbooks, missals, or even the life of some saint. *Real* books.

My choice, I grant, is not easily explained. Let us therefore leave it unexplained. I bought a book on cave exploring whose name escapes me, and *First on the Rope*, by Roger Frison-Roche. An abyss and a summit . . . I read the novel on mountain climbing immediately, that very evening, and thoroughly enjoyed it. It was confiscated the moment I came back to school, for on leafing through it the good ladies of the Sodality discovered not only a tale of masculine endurance but a very brief love story, too.

The next morning I set out in search of the school, in order to meet the priest. The porter did not show me into the little parlor off the entry hall but into the teachers' workroom. I felt instantly at home there: the studious atmosphere, the piles of work on the tables, and above all, the music playing softly on the radio. Learning had an entirely different air about it here from what it had at Montluçon. Was I, too, going to become a "*jèʒe*"? Could I, too, belong to this elite someday? That was exactly what I wanted that morning, and I later spoke to Father L. about it. Three years' more schooling, and then the novitiate. The path was already laid out: what elation!

Father L. suggested a walk. After strolling briefly through the streets of the town, we entered a church. It was a gloomy day and the stained-glass windows let no light through: in the choir, however, on both sides of the altar, the little flames of dozens of candles gave an air of unreality to this not particularly beautiful church.

We had circled the nave in no time, but we halted in one of the side chapels, talking in low voices of the war and of my parents, and contemplating a picture of Christ on the Cross, so shadowed that even in the flickering light of the candles one could see nothing but a face and a body, as though they were suspended in a void. "Didn't your parents die at Auschwitz?" Father L. asked. What did this name mean? Where was Auschwitz? He must have understood then that I knew almost nothing of the extermination of the Jews. To me, the death of my parents was enveloped in vague images, indistinct circumstances that bore no relation to the real course of events. And so, in front of this obscure Christ, I listened: Auschwitz, the trains, the gas chambers, the crematory ovens, the millions of dead . . .

When we got back to the school, Father L. read a few pages of an autobiographical text in which a historian who was a French

Jew describes how, when still a child, he discovered anti-Semitism for the first time. Whom was he reading? I am unable to say today, but all through this decisive day I had the impression that the essential pieces of a puzzle that heretofore had made no sense were falling into place.

For the first time, I felt myself to be Jewish — no longer despite myself or secretly, but through a sensation of absolute loyalty. It is true that I knew nothing of Judaism and was still a Catholic. But something had changed. A tie had been reestablished, an identity was emerging, a confused one certainly, contradictory perhaps, but from that day forward linked to a central axis of which there could be no doubt: in some manner or other I was Jewish — whatever this term meant in my mind.

The attitude of Father L. himself profoundly influenced me: to hear him speak of the lot of the Jews with so much emotion and respect must have been an important encouragement for me. He did not press me to choose one path or the other — and perhaps he would have preferred to see me remain Catholic — but his sense of justice (or was it a profound charity?) led him to recognize my right to judge for myself, by helping me to renew the contact with my past.

I do not have the slightest recollection of the return to Montluçon, and yet how moved I must have been, and how confused my thoughts! So I was fully Jewish, but I was also a Catholic and, at that time, quite determined to remain one. How, then, to reconcile the two, how, above all, to know what it meant to be Jewish?

I could only have had a very vague notion of Jewishness, an image composed of the most disparate elements: Jewish origins obviously, the children of Montmorency and those of La

Souterraine, Fraenkel and his jokes, the story of Hanukkah, the usurer Abraham, the murderers of Christ, Bergson too, and now Auschwitz and the long trail of persecutions and deaths; the image of our death . . .

Wasn't it madness to identify with my Jewishness when Paul-Henri Ferland had no remaining link to the Jews? For I could now remain a Catholic, without the slightest hesitation: hadn't my ties with the past disappeared forever? I dreamed endlessly of my future as a priest and was convinced of my vocation. So where did this need of a return, a return toward a decimated, humiliated, miserable group, come from? Had I been born of a "really" Jewish family, I would at least have had coherent memories, but in my case this inner obstacle, this constant reminder played no role: I was free.

What secret work was accomplished within me during this trip? What instinct, buried beneath acquired loyalty, suddenly caused a profounder loyalty to emerge? An obscure rupture, brought about by the astonishing discovery at Saint-Étienne.

When I returned to Saint-Béranger, I asked people to stop using my borrowed name and reassumed the name that was mine.

Three or four months after my return from Saint-Étienne, I left Saint-Béranger forever to join my guardian and his family. Just as the details of my arrival at Montluçon were erased from my mind, so the memory of my departure has become blurred. In my heart of hearts I still feel a strange attraction, mingled with a profound repulsion, for this phase of my childhood. It was twenty-five years after my departure before I decided to take the road to Néris-les-Bains and the rue de la Garde again. I was accompanied by my son Eli, who had just turned ten.

Part III

October 24, 1977

Classes have begun again. Students are soaking up sunshine on the lawn in front of the seminar room; at the entrance to the library there is the usual busy traffic back and forth that marks the beginning of a school year. The atmosphere is peaceful. Everywhere, however, dozens of khaki patches mingle with the loud colors of shirts and the faded blue of jeans: uniforms.

The seminar addresses itself to a long-standing preoccupation: what is the importance of myths in our societies? Long immobile, charged with contained force, they nonetheless remain alive. We know they are ready to surface again, to spread, like a trail of flame, or like torrents that unexpectedly fill dry ravines and sweep down across the plains, carrying off everything in their wake. For us, too, there is the enormous, continuous presence of myths . . .

Anyway, what are the values being transmitted here? The faces look young, but many of these students have participated in at least one war . . .

And what are the values that I myself can transmit? Can experience as personal, as contradictory as mine rouse an echo here, in even the most indirect way? I am not sure. But must I then limit myself to the neutral indifference of the technician, or alternatively, pretend that I have roots, play at normality, and return to clear thoughts, those which help one to live and, perhaps, to die? Isn't the way out for me to attach myself to the necessary order, the inescapable simplification forced upon one by the passage of time and one's vision of history, to adopt the gaze of the historian?

In 1961, four years after my stay in Sweden, I finally started back on the road to the university. Through the shifting prism of eyewitness accounts, stories, documents in archives, I tried to grasp the meaning of a period and reestablish the coherency of a past, my own. Through interviews as well. And so it was that at the end of 1962 I left for Aumühle, in northern Germany near the Danish frontier, to meet there the man who had commanded the German navy and after Hitler's suicide had become, for just a few days, the head of a Reich in ruins, ex-Grand Admiral Dönitz, sentenced to ten years' imprisonment by the Nuremberg Tribunal.

I left Switzerland in the early hours of the morning and planned on ending my journey very late at night. When I reached Mannheim the peaceful, unshadowed landscape that slipped by on both sides of the road suddenly began to look different to me. I would not call it anxiety or panic, but a strange feeling of desolation came upon me: this Autobahn was shutting me up in Germany forever; on every hand were Germans, nothing but Germans. I felt caught in a blind trap. In the ponderous cars going past me, the faces seemed to be suddenly bloated with a rancid, reddish grease; on the shoulder of the road the signs — in German! — represented so many cold injunctions, issued by an all-powerful, destructive, police-state bureaucracy.

Since then I have often returned to Germany. More than once, the same sensation has come over me, though less intense and more complex. On the one hand, danger, a trap, desolation; but at the same time a feeling of familiarity, pleasant familiarity: the language, the streets, the songs, the waters of the Rhine that I had seen only once, at Kehl, the hillsides covered with grapevines, the old castles and the baroque churches — everything was thoroughly familiar to me. And so, at the archives in Bonn, Koblenz, or Freiburg, I would read my records, those of the Ministry of Foreign Affairs of the Reich, those of the Ministry of Propaganda, and others; but when night came, how many times have I hesitated between the attractions of a *Weinstube* as familiar as everything else and the imperative need to pack my suitcases immediately, flee instantly, go back across the border at all costs . . .

It was only at this time in my life, when I was around thirty, that I realized how much the past molded my vision of things, how much the essential appeared to me through a particular prism that could never be eliminated. But did it have to be eliminated? A great number of us go through life this way, insensible to a whole range of shades and tones, though, despite everything, the eye still manages to penetrate, in certain situations, far beyond the neutral, aseptic, normal meanings that reality presents. If our reactions may sometimes seem strange, let there be no mistake about it: behind the harmless surface of words and things, we know that at any and every moment abysses await us.

I have a precise memory of my conversation with Admiral Doenitz, but it is as though it has been transposed into fantasy. He received me at nightfall, sitting at a massive desk. Behind him, large windows overlooked a garden. The daylight was fading; no one turned on the lights in the room, and soon we were talking in twilight.

"I assure you that I knew nothing about the extermination of the Jews."

Words, phrases, denials. I was tired all of a sudden, tired in advance. Did one only have to deny the past, deny it steadfastly, in order for that past to disappear forever? What was I doing here, in front of this enigmatic man, who was not going to give me so much as a glimpse of the world I was seeking to unveil?

It was almost dark now and the narrow halo of light that illuminated the desk gave the figure, the room, the interview a vaguely fantastic quality.

"Sir, can you give me your word of honor as a German grand admiral that you knew nothing?"

The response came immediately, clipped words without a shadow of hesitation: "I give you my word of honor as a German grand admiral that I knew nothing."

A few months ago I saw Joachim Fest's film, *Hitler: A Career*, in a movie theater in Munich. The dazzling rise, the titanic energy, the Luciferian fall: it is all there. As for the extermination of the Jews, a few words in passing, no more. An inconsequential shadow on this grandiose tableau. For anyone who does not know the facts, the power and the glory still remain, followed by a veritable vengeance of the gods; or the long roll calls in the night, in front of the Feldherrnhalle,* illuminated by thousands of torches, draped in flags bearing the swastika:

"Felix Alfahrth!"

"Present!"

"Andreas Bauriedl!"

"Present!"

. . .

For anyone who does not know the facts, the mystical communion with the brownshirt revolution and its martyrs still remains.

---

*The Feldherrnhalle (Field Commanders' Hall) is a nineteenth-century monumental loggia on Odeonsplatz in Munich. During the Third Reich it became the site of an annual commemoration for the sixteen Nazis killed at that location by the police during Hitler's failed Beer Hall Putsch of November 1923.

Thus is evidence transformed over the years, thus do memories crumble away.

On leaving Montluçon I was going to discover "life" and "the world," between the walls of a dusty provincial school and in the family of a small Jewish tradesman, my "surrogate guardian."

Curiously enough, when I think back on it now, I discover a certain poetry in the streets of our little town, bordered with uneven sidewalks and narrow gutters; during summer afternoons, one could slowly count the number of passersby. The greenish waters of the stagnant pools that appeared here and there amid the gardens as soon as one left the center of town seem to me not without charm, and even the old women, all dressed in black, who sat for hours on their doorsteps without moving, bring to mind an element of stability and permanence. This provincial France was archaic, primitive, old-fashioned; it was also stable and firmly rooted. How I sometimes envy the unconscious tranquillity of such immobility! What a difference from the world I had glimpsed in Prague, and from the one I was about to discover!

My new guardian and his wife had come to France as Russian immigrants during the twenties; on the eve of the war, they had a prosperous business selling textiles in the fourth arrondissement in Paris. But the beginnings, as I understand it, were difficult: they had to go from door to door, along the narrow streets of the Marais, samples in hand, convert their apartment into a warehouse, drag rolls of cotton or sateen up four floors and stack them up in unstable heaps in the corridors, the bedroom, and even the kitchen. And above all, they had to hang on, despite fluctuations or crises in the economic situation, so as finally to make their own, albeit modest, place in the sun. The arrival of the Germans swept everything away, though they managed to escape persecution; but when I arrived, my guardian and his family were still leading a very precarious existence.

During the academic year, I was a boarder at the school; on Sundays, though, and during vacations, I was invited by my new guardian to stay with him.

I have often thought since about this family, about the type of Jews it represented: there, before me, was the Russo-Polish stock that, in a word, made Israel. An image comes to mind when I think of them, a strange image but a true one, it seems to me, that of ivy. To cling: such might have been their motto. To cling to rocks, to bare walls, to the most arid surface. And it matters little whether a branch is cut off or a plant divided; the foliage is soon as thick and vigorous as before. Ivy: symbol of vitality and tenacity.

I felt entirely out of my element. The passage from Saint-Béranger to my new setting was truly that from one world to another, with no point of contact, no possible association. My guardian's family in no way resembled my own, either; in fact, it represented the very opposite of the background of my early childhood. Instead of culture and refinement, a rough-and-ready, somewhat primitive vitality; instead of reserve and carefully controlled emotions, and the apparent coldness I have spoken of, a noisy exuberance, very soon carried to extremes; instead of the almost total absence of a Jewish tradition, an atmosphere saturated with Jewish emotions, allusions, customs, mannerisms.

My guardian was a religious man. When I happened to stay overnight *en famille*, I would see him, early in the morning, drape the prayer shawl around him, place his phylacteries on his forehead, roll the strips of leather around his arms, and plunge into the recitation of his prayers at a dizzying speed. In the beginning, after the pomp and ceremony of the big chapel, this sort of devotions seemed ridiculous to me. But eventually I became used to it and even came to feel how authentic the familiar, informal side of Jewish prayer can be. But this was later.

In fact, I am calling up echoes of the atmosphere of a shtetl, a little Jewish settlement in Eastern Europe, colored, of course, by the contact with a French province, but still a shtetl atmosphere that stemmed from yet another characteristic: poverty. Easier times were to return, but because of external constraints, this immediate postwar period greatly resembled the old days in the little communities of Poland and Russia. Thus I could not say whether we had running water, but I do know that the toilet was in an outdoor shed, at the back of a little yard half invaded by brambles, and if this presented few problems in summer, I would not wish the inevitable long waits over a hole in winter on anyone.

One night that winter, when the cold became too much to bear, my guardian and I slept in the same bed in order to make the use of the blankets more rational. In Prague, I always slept in my room alone; in Rochlitz, too. I have recounted how, moved by fear, I would get up at night to see if my father was still there, near the tall standing lamp in the living room, but I have not mentioned the pillow that at this time in my life I considered the most faithful and intimate of companions. Being alone became tolerable thanks to the presence of my pillow. On my fourth birthday my father came into my bedroom and said, "You're a big boy now and you don't need this pillow any more." I tried to defend my rights, to no avail; the pillow was confiscated.

This detour, via these vignettes, has brought me back to two well-nigh incompatible categories: those people who stay close to each other, who like common warmth, and the others, who avoid contact, keep their distance, refuse to indulge in any sort of promiscuity, sentimentality, or excessive enthusiasm. If one concedes that these are two fundamental attitudes toward life, two attitudes that go beyond trivial, everyday problems, then it is obvious — as I have already said — that our country was built by the first type, by the enthusiasts, those who are elated by common warmth. They move forward with passion, but also blindly, for an irresistible attraction always brings them back to a common center: life and the vision of the group. The world around them is there only to reflect their own image of things; the world around them, in effect, does not exist.

November 12, 1977

There are evenings when the city suddenly disappears beneath a thick layer of clouds or mist. In the orange halo of the streetlights one can see frayed wisps of fog crowd past, as though some great piece of news were drawing them toward an invisible meeting place, far off in the east. Weather that favors mystery and daydreaming. Nonetheless, Jerusalem, at once the city of history and of eternity, is not a city of legends. Here there is no Golem who paces down dark little back streets. It makes one think that legends cannot flourish at the source of all legends, or that everything here must contribute to what is essential.

People did their best to give me back a perfect Jewish identity as soon as possible. I accepted these attempts, so long as they did not run counter to my "conscience." Hence I attended the services on Yom Kippur, but what I remember most clearly was a rainy evening, a little hall where we were all crowded together, and the smell of wet woolen clothing, rather than the accents of the Kol Nidre. In short, an uneventful Yom Kippur. But how can

I ever forget, on the other hand, the Passover dinner, the traditional Seder, of the following spring?

The whole family had just come back to Paris and was gathered once again in the apartment near Saint-Paul. It was understood that I was to join them there for the holiday. On the appointed day I set out. The night train, the Gare d'Austerlitz, the Métro to the Saint-Paul station: I was really back in Paris.

There were at least fifteen of us: every friend left in the city was there with us. The table with its multiple extra leaves occupied the entire length of the living room. The number of guests, the gleaming silverware, the candles: everything contributed to the festive air.

We read the Haggadah, commented on the traditional verses, compared the events recounted with present-day reality, raised our glasses four times as required by the rite — in a word, we celebrated the exodus from Egypt . . .

Two years later I was to participate in my first Seder in Israel, at the Ben Shemen school. The celebration of the holiday had lost its traditional air there; the reading of the Haggadah had been replaced by modern texts, and the prayers by songs of our own day. But the commemoration, the deep feeling, and the symbols were the same: we celebrated the freedom from bondage, the end of a dark era, the dawn of a new time. Yet the traditional celebration, such as I experienced it for the first time in the home of my guardian — and very often subsequently — seemed to me to be the only really meaningful one: it is the holy words, repeated over the centuries, that give the general symbol its particular force, that mark the sinking of roots in a group, the sinking of roots in history and in time. Because they have never been entirely clear, and always open to exegesis and explanation, it is the holy words that open the doors of imagination and allow the humblest of participants to understand, in his own way, the story and the feeling of liberation, knowing that these traditional words are his anchor and foundation within the community.

Nothing of all this was evident to me when I took my place at the table for this first Seder; I did not realize that for me, too, in a certain sense, this was a freedom that had been rediscovered. And hence the incident that today gives rise to a smile but that at the time provoked consternation. The meal began. When the soup was served I partook of it without a word, but when the pièces de résistance arrived, the meat in particular, I excused myself. Surprise: "Aren't you feeling well?" "No, I feel fine." "Well, come on, eat then!" I continued to say no and was obliged to explain myself: "Well, it's like this, you see; it's Good Friday today, and I can't eat meat . . ."

This first stay in Paris after the war lasted as long as it took me to enroll at the Lycée Henri IV. It made me proud, but also vaguely ill at ease, to think that when the school year began I would be a pupil in this prestigious school. I awaited the month of October impatiently and fearfully.

One afternoon I found myself, without having really so intended, on the rue Montholon, near the hotel in which my parents and I had stayed when we first arrived in Paris. I couldn't go in. For some time, I wandered about the neighborhood, then went back toward the *grands boulevards*, headed down the boulevard des Italiens, and found our milk bar. This time I did not hesitate. I ordered our favorite milk shake, a strawberry one. In days long past, my mother used to help me climb up onto the stool and I never felt quite safe perched up there. The stool now scarcely reached my waist. The counterman pours the foamy drink into a tall glass with the same free, easy, elegant gesture as long ago. Is he going to give me a straw? I suck through it. The same sweet taste, of course, and the iridescent bubbles burst at the edges of the glass just as they did long ago. The mirrors on the wall haven't changed, nor have the moleskin banquettes. And yet this milk shake, though it brings back memories, doesn't summon up what I am looking for . . . No, really not . . . And I sit there at a loss, in front of this cool drink, pleasant in the first warmth of spring, while all around me, slowly, the dusty brightness of a beautiful April day flows by.

In this same period I was obliged to go to Bourges several times. My guardian knew a Jewish tailor there who for a rather modest sum was willing to alter my father's suits to fit me. These brief journeys remain clear in my mind, not so much because of my visits to the cathedral as because of the hours spent at the tailor's.

He lived in a small apartment, on the ground floor of an old house near the park; the windows of the living room, which was also his workroom, overlooked a large square that was almost always empty. He lived there with a daughter my age, a sweet, unaffected girl who seldom said anything. After the usual fittings, I would sit down in one corner, the tailor's daughter would sit near the window with a book on her knees, and the father would bend over his work and speak monosyllables in an even tone of voice. I liked the calm, the monotony, even, of these moments. I would look out at the square through the long-unwashed window-panes, and sometimes steal furtive glances at the girl, who with no less hesitation would glance back at me, and I would let myself be gently lulled by the rhythm of sounds that were always quiet ones, whether it was the tailor's voice, the staccato of the sewing machine, the almost imperceptible creak of the scissors on the fabric, or the intermittent buzzing of a fly.

A very old memory, perhaps my earliest, came back to me. I must have been no more than three and was sitting in our kitchen at Rochlitz. My mother wasn't there, nor Vlasta either, but my grandmother Cécile (or Cili, as we called her) was busy at the stove. I could hear her talking, I could hear the little repeated sounds of a wooden spoon tapping the sides of a pot and in the background the noise of flies circling the immense table; from time to time a brief silence announced that one of them had just gotten stuck on the ribbon of yellow flypaper, already studded with black dots, which hung from one of the beams overhead.

At my guardian's, recent events were one subject of our conversations. For instance, near our little city the Vichy militia — or was it Germans? — had flung some thirty Jews into a well and then crushed them to death beneath a pile of stones they threw in after them. Of these stories, those dealing with the camps themselves naturally impressed me more than all the rest. The names of Belzec and Maidanek struck me particularly. I wanted to write.

One Saturday night after dinner, everyone left for the movies except me. I contemplated the oilcloth on the dinner table, still covered with crumbs and spots of grease, then stared at the damp spots on the wallpaper. I was trying to hypnotize myself somehow, to put myself in a different state so that the first words of a poem would burst forth from me. But nothing happened. The spots remained spots, and Belzec and Maidanek disappeared in a distant fog, despite the various things that I could call to mind. It was only much later, on thinking about these efforts, that I understood that what was missing was not literary talent but rather a certain ability to identify. The veil between events and me had not been rent. I had lived on the edges of the catastrophe; a distance — impassable, perhaps — separated me from those who had been directly caught up in the tide of events, and despite all my efforts, I remained, in my own eyes, not so much a victim as — a spectator. I was destined, therefore, to wander among several worlds, knowing them, understanding them — better, perhaps, than many others — but nonetheless incapable of feeling an identification without any reticence, incapable of seeing, understanding, and belonging in a single, immediate, total movement. Hence — need I say? — my enormous difficulty in writing this book.

November 18, 1977

Ten days ago, the news seemed to be one of those attractive but empty formulas that ornament the grayness of everyday life: President Sadat had declared that he was prepared to come to Jerusalem; last Tuesday we began to believe that it was true; yesterday brought certainty, enthusiasm, incontrovertible fact: the president of Egypt would be arriving in Israel in two days, on Saturday night. Something was changing, not only in the Middle East, not only in the conflict between the Arab world and us, but something in the very course of our history.

For twelve years I had been instinctively making calculations in spite of myself. When Eli turned six, I said to myself: "This is how old I was when I left Prague, how old I was when I went off to Montmorency; his life is still all right." When he turned ten, I couldn't help but think that at the age of ten . . . I did the same thing with David, and then with little Michal; Michal is seven now, and things are all right . . . But Eli is almost eighteen and in a few months it will be the army, daily anxiety, endless discussions of news broadcasts, the imperceptible start when the telephone rings . . . Maybe all that will change now.

It never ceases to surprise me how quickly night falls here. It is barely five o'clock and already it is almost dark outside. The lights have been turned on everywhere. I imagine that, like me, hundreds of thousands of people are waiting with growing impatience for the Sabbath to go by.

Saturday, November 19 – Monday, November 21, 1977

For several days, a hundred yards from my house, the flags flew side by side: the three colors of Egypt and the blue Star of David on a white background. The curious onlookers have dispersed; I, the last of them, stay and look. On both sides these flags have led enemies into battle; on both sides thousands of men have died for these flags. Today one and the same wind, one and the same breath of air stirs them . . . In the distance, the hills seem to stand out more sharply than usual; despite the season, the air has the softness of spring; all over the city, one can feel an atmosphere of rejoicing, the first stirrings of a joy thus far unknown, a new joy mounting . . .

My guardian was the first to speak to me of Eretz Israel. When I left the school and came to spend a day at his house, I was often transported to far-distant places: by way of the interminable discussions, as in the pages of *La Terre retrouvée* (*The Homeland Regained*), I discovered the realities of "Eretz," as it was called, "the homeland."

One of my first memories of this time is that of the deep emotion aroused in us by the events of Black Saturday, the day when the British forces, after the acts of sabotage by the Haganah, arrested almost all the political leaders of the Jewish community. The British foreign secretary, Ernest Bevin, had become our bête noire, and General Barker, the commander of the British forces in Palestine, struck us as being a sort of Himmler, since he had said that he would punish the Jews in a way this race disliked most of all, "by striking at their pocket and showing our contempt for them."

An Anglo-American commission had recommended that Palestine be opened to a hundred thousand Jewish refugees who were still living in camps in Europe, but the British government stubbornly refused. A terrorist group, Menachem Begin's Irgun, blew up the King David Hotel in Jerusalem, burying about a hundred civil servants and British officers beneath the ruins. Lightning strikes and reprisals followed each other without respite. During this time thousands of Jews left the camps in Germany and Austria and headed for Italian ports. Old tubs, chartered by the Haganah, tried, by any and every means, to reach the coast of Palestine in secret. From week to week, from month to month, we lived through all the developments of this struggle. The illegal vessels arrived in sight of Eretz Israel. Intercepted by the Royal Navy, they tried through passive resistance to force the British to let their passengers land. Most of the refugees were driven off and sometimes taken back to European ports, and even to Germany, as in the case of the *Exodus*. Soon camps in Cyprus took the place of the European ones. The doors of Palestine remained closed; a great drama was unfolding beneath our eyes.

In 1946, on the eve of Yom Kippur, President Truman once again demanded that more than a hundred thousand refugees be authorized to enter Palestine, and for the first time he alluded to the possibility of creating a Jewish state. A Jewish state.

Roth and a few other neighbors would sometimes drop in to see us, and despite the Yiddish they spoke, I would follow, without losing a single word, the interminable debates, dotted with the strangest conjectures, on the course of events in Eretz Israel. One glass of tea followed another, and I never ceased to be astonished by the way they kept the lumps of sugar in their mouths instead of putting them in the glass. That was how tea was drunk in Plonsk or Brest-Litovsk.

What did I think Eretz Israel was like? I am quite certain I put together the most diverse elements to form a single vision of it:

the two or three images inherited from my own past — Haifa and, above all, Tel Aviv and the taste of caramel (with the very white houses and the very blue sea of the postcards my mother sent). Superimposed on these very first images are those evoked by my guardian's stories: in them oranges and grapefruit are intermingled with proud blond heroes and model farms, which were how I pictured the kibbutzim, and vague-looking caches of arms from which would come surprises and deliverance.

With such pictures, which were simplistic to say the least, in my mind, I was sent in August 1946 to a vacation camp for Zionist youth on the shores of Lake Chalain, in the Jura Mountains. As a matter of course, I was put with the Habonim (the Builders), a socialist group.

It was at Chalain that an inner rift, till then almost imperceptible, began to manifest itself. It is not my intention here to simplify the image and present, as an example to be followed, the story of a descent and a return to the surface. Those who descend never return altogether to the surface.

The imprint of Saint-Béranger was not without importance, and aside from the "cases of conscience" that I have already spoken of, it forced me, for at least a year, to remain on my guard. At Chalain, for example, as in my provincial city, I went to the movies only twice: to see *Battle of the Rails* and *The Last Chance*. Apart from that, I had to avoid, acrobatically, all invitations, for, preoccupied as I still was by "bad thoughts" and "traps of the Devil," how would I have dared even approach a movie theater where they were showing, let us say, *Madonna of the Sleeping Cars*? And when my tentmate took out his harmonica and began to play "The Blue Danube," gesturing to me to sing the tune so he could accompany me, it was quite hard for me to say, in an offhand way, that my voice was hoarse, thus hiding the fact that I had never heard of Strauss and his waltzes before.

These were only passing troubles; the rest has to do with something essential. Several times a week after dinner there were campfires, and late into the night anyone on the other shore of the lake could then hear, above the motionless black waters, the strains of "Hevenu Shalom Aleichem," "Bei mir bist du schön," or "Crocuses in the meadow, it is the end of summer . . ."

I liked "Crocuses in the meadow," but despite what I had felt at La Souterraine when I heard Yiddish or Hebrew songs, I did not feel at ease. Whereas in the light of the slowly dying flames, my companions' faces seemed illuminated from within by this familiar music, this music of homes and firesides and childhood which quite naturally led to new songs about Eretz Israel, I, though I hummed along with the others, was vaguely aware that the mask of an outsider concealed my innermost nature. What this innermost nature was I would not have been able to say.

Thus, though it was no doubt unusual, I did not become a Zionist by way of a renewal of contact with buried emotional layers, but rather as a result of logical argument, of a simple line of reasoning that nonetheless in those days seemed to me to be a compelling one.

During one of those late nights, one of the camp counselors, Sigi, began to hold forth. For me he shed a new light on recent events: he spoke of the passivity of the victims. Why this passivity? We felt at home nowhere, we found help nowhere. But all this was over and done with: we would never go to the slaughter like a herd of sheep again! And in order to bring this about we needed a state. Within the framework of a state, we could take our fate in our own hands; only within the framework of a state could we answer violence with force . . .

Autumn crocuses in the meadow, it is the end of summer.

The message of Chalain had an immediate and unexpected effect. Two weeks after I returned from vacation, I entered our town school as a boarder. As I really didn't look at all like the boys from the region, I was naturally chosen as the target for systematic hazing. On the second night, shortly after I fell asleep, my bed collapsed beneath me; the bolts of its joints had been unscrewed. I had been taken by surprise; I decided not to let it happen a second time. Didn't we have to abandon our role as victims, didn't we have to answer violence with force, even if the Jewish state was still only a dream? Without the slightest hesitation, I identified my personal situation with that of the community: I was prepared to confront our enemies, weapons in hand! And so I did. As soon as the dormitory master turned out the lights the next night, I tied a stone, prepared in advance, to the end of my belt, and when the enemy approached my bed on hands and knees, I struck out with all my strength.

2

When the train pulled out of the Gare de Lyon, I finally believed that what was happening to me was real. Outside the window the gray buildings of a nearby suburb filed by, and in the compartment passengers were still stirring as they settled down for the long trip. The idea finally penetrated my mind: high school was over, the waiting was over, far-off dreams were over. I was leaving to fight in Eretz Israel; I was fifteen years old.

Now rows of smaller houses, surrounded by gardens, were flying past on each side of the track, and the streetlights had just come on. Night was falling; the train was picking up speed. Long train trips like this had divided my brief existence into distinct areas, separated by deep rifts: the journey from Prague to Paris, the one from Paris to Néris, the one from Montluçon to Saint-Étienne, and then the return from my provincial city to Paris. And now I was on my way to Marseilles, where the greatest of my adventures was about to begin. I think I share with many others my attraction for railway stations, for tracks that stretch out to infinity, for the red and green lights of the signals, for everything that expresses the melancholy of departures mingled with the dreams aroused by great changes...

Just a few months before, when I left my province and arrived in Paris to enter the top class, section A, at the Lycée Henri IV as a boarder, who would have predicted the change I was now experiencing? The immediate path before me seemed already mapped out: at the end of the year I would take the first baccalaureate examination, and then I would have a final year of philosophy and the second *bac*. If I passed — about which I had no serious doubts — for me the next stage was self-evident: preparatory classes and the competitive entrance examination for the École Normale. Such was the height of my ambition, at any rate, when classes started up again in the fall of 1947. Since my guardian was able to provide only the bare necessities, I was about to become a "ward of the nation," and then a French national. What more could anyone in my position desire?

During the week I seldom went outside the four walls of my school, except to buy a newspaper in the mornings and bread for a snack in the afternoons. On Thursdays and Sundays I went to my guardian's, and sometimes to the meetings of the Communist Youth cell of the fifth arrondissement, to one or another of the big political demonstrations of those days, and of course to the meetings organized by the Habonim. As for my Catholicism, it had almost disappeared.

It would be hard for me today to point to any particular reason for this transformation, if indeed anything more than time, the pressure of my surroundings, and the usual turmoil of adolescence was at work. Shortly before the end of the vacation that preceded my arrival in Paris, I saw Father L. again, at Lyons this time, in the Jesuit house at Fourvières, but this second meeting had no particular effect on me: I remained aloof.

I cannot help wondering, as I mention this change, what has remained of this education, in the completely different world that became mine. On the deepest level, nothing, as I have already said. But perhaps a certain unease in my relationships with people, a reticence that the rue de la Garde and its taboos inculcated, no doubt permanently. And, moreover, the beginnings of a tendency, nourished by other sources as well, to passivity rather than action, to moral preoccupations and ponderings rather than a cold acceptance of reality. In short, a certain difficulty in living that hinders spontaneity but encourages constant self-examination, continual dissatisfaction; an attitude that resembles, moreover, a particular Jewish one, that of Jews on the way to assimilation, caught between two worlds: the milieu in which we had lived. Thus in the end everything converges.

I came naturally to Communism, or nearly so — could one be young in those days without being a Communist? My Zionist convictions were strengthened as a result of this change: in 1947 the Communists were calling for the creation of a Jewish state in Palestine. This was not without a certain comic element, for my mentor in Communism and my support in Zionism was none other than one of my neighbors in the dormitory and the study hall at the time, a student with a brilliant mind, later destined to have a splendid career as a theoretician of neo-Marxist economics: the Egyptian Samir Amin. Hence I read *The Poverty of Philosophy* and discussed the thought of the Zionist Ber Borochov with this elder of mine in our math class, who in appearance at least seemed to be directly descended from Tutankhamen. Samir, it is true, did not accompany me to meetings of the Habonim, whereas I for my part went, as I have just said, to those of the fifth arrondissement Communist Youth cell and above all to demonstrations. I have very bad memories of these latter.

At the end of the year the CGT (the central trade union organization) called a series of insurrectional strikes, affecting even the high schools: a strike of employees in the supply office that forced us to make the rounds of university restaurants, strikes of classroom assistants, and so on. We marched, from the Place de la République to the Bastille, from the Place de la Nation to I don't remember where. Like everyone else, I learned to sing the "Internationale" and acclaimed Maurice Thorez in one of the great stadiums of the capital.

One day I was given the task of selling *L'Humanité*. But, timid as I was, I felt incapable of shouting "Buy *L'Huma*!" — with the result that at a demonstration attended by at least fifty thousand people I sold only five or six papers: I slipped them, with a vague whisper, into the hands of the people around me, as though they were some sort of forbidden pamphlet or pornographic picture. It was after this experience, I think, that I began to move away from Communism.

There remained Zionism. I made of it, at this point, the most important thing in my life.

. . . The train was now rushing through open country. I should have known who my traveling companions were, all of them two or three years older than I; in fact, I came to know their names and faces for the first time on the train. These names and faces have disappeared from my memory today, with the exception of those of my neighbor on the left, Ruth; she left me with a memory of gentleness.

I cannot say today what ideas raced through my head at the time, but I remember clearly that during the first part of the trip, once we had settled down, what aroused my joy and my happy expectations much more than the distant prospect of arriving in Eretz was the certainty that in a few hours I would have my first glimpse of the sea.

On our television screens, surprising images from Cairo: "I am from Israeli television . . ." That is how our reporter introduces himself to people in the streets of the Egyptian capital: the welcome is cordial, even enthusiastic at times. But will we ever believe in peace? Will we ever be able to envisage our future from a perspective of peace? Since the beginning of its history, this people has seen itself as alone and surrounded by enemies, and has been incapable of faith in anything save its God and then its destiny. For centuries, misfortune and catastrophe have always seemed to be the most imminent eventualities, though the trust in ultimate deliverance has never entirely disappeared. Our identity is linked to this vision of the world and of the future. Is it possible for these almost atavistic attitudes to evaporate from one day to the next? I listen to the comments around me: for many, peace seems to have become a certainty; the weight of the past has suddenly turned out to have a strange, unexpected lightness.

Yesterday I met H., who lost a son during the most recent war. I can guess what he is thinking. *Why now and not four years ago?* There is no bitterness apparent in what he says, however. He seems to be living the same hope as all of us. But an almost imperceptible hesitation accompanies his words at times and now and again his eyes grow veiled, as though they no longer see, as though his gaze were turned inward, toward some invisible point. What does peace mean to him?

From the autumn of 1947 Zionism became my principal occupation. That in no way prevented me, however, from living the usual life of a schoolboy, save for a few details.

After my arrival in Paris, for instance, I almost never had any pocket money; even paying for a haircut presented a problem. This nonetheless did not stand in my way. One day I went into a barbershop on the boulevard Saint-Michel, a few steps away from the Lycée Saint-Louis, without a sou in my pocket; I nevertheless imperturbably asked for a haircut. Let destiny take its course. I waited, and as I left my chair I spied a sign reading WET PAINT posted in a not very visible place. The solution was there before me, as easy as pie: a spot of paint on my jacket, furious protests, explanations, apologies, and the inevitable compromise: I wouldn't pay the barber, and he for his part wouldn't have my jacket cleaned. We were even.

The fare for Paris boarding students in those postwar years was not copious; far from it. My schoolmates eked out their daily meals with personal provisions; myself, I had a hollow ache in my belly most of the time. On Sundays I sometimes ate at my guardian's; I also sometimes entered a café, ordered croissants and hot milk, swallowed them down, and skipped out at a run without paying.

To tell the truth, I have often been hungry. Not in Prague, certainly. Those first years left me with memories of abundance. Everyone knows our national dishes, the *knedliki* of all sorts that for generations have made the reputation of both Czech and Viennese cuisine, but do you have any idea what "Indians," sold in the pastry shops of the Old City, were? Balls of chocolate, split in two and filled with whipped cream . . . As for family repasts in Prague, a week never went by without a roast goose or turkey being served, its flesh larded with fat and the inside filled with a rich stuffing; paradise, in short. One curious detail: after the failure of our attempt to leave the country by car, we met together once more at a dinner of this sort; the traditional goose sat smoking on the table, as though nothing had happened. It is hard for me to understand such feasts today; looking backward doubtless distorts one's vision.

Later on, good things to eat disappeared from my life. I have mentioned my first reactions to the food served at Saint-Béranger. I eventually became accustomed to it. During recess, casein biscuits were handed out to us, a Red Cross contribution to the health of French children. Sometimes we used to go to the Sodality's vegetable garden at the other end of the city, to work there and to march in religious processions. I remember one of these exercises in piety that came while the plum trees were covered with fruit. Like all the others, I moved forward with my eyes glued to the statue of the Virgin, but the flesh is weak, and, a budding Saint Anthony, I saw appear before my eyes, not lascivious temptresses, but fat purple plums that I imagined were as juicy as could be wished for. I was properly repentant.

After the war I received a package from America. My father had had two faithful friends who, after crossing the ocean just in time, lost interest in our fate. One of them, however, sent me this package. It was a feast. There were only three or four of us at Saint-Béranger that summer. A table was set out in the little courtyard near the gate, from where I had run away to the hospital, and the precious package was placed precisely in the center of it. I can still see us feeling, weighing, admiring everything that Madame Robert extracted from it, piece by piece, like so many marvels pulled out of a magician's hat. After a while I could control myself no longer: in front of me was a shining cube vaguely recalling the caramels of yesteryear. My hand reached out, and I popped it into my mouth. It was a bouillon cube . . .

We were very proud, I think, of belonging to our prestigious lycée and we admired the elegance of the quadrangle topped by the Tour Saint-Jacques, whose pure lines complemented the celebrated lineaments of the Place du Panthéon. We had our crazes, too. On Thursdays and Sundays, for instance, I would sometimes accompany Philippe A. to a *discothèque*, on the corner of the boulevard Saint-Michel and the rue Soufflot — not a *discothèque* where you danced, but one of those where you listened to records on slot machines, with earphones. When I had a few sous, I religiously dialed the same numbers each time, clapped the earphones over my ears, and, close to ecstasy, awaited the first chords of the overture to *Tannhäuser* or "The Ride of the Valkyries." In the evening in the dormitory, one of us would whistle the glissando of the violins of the "Venusberg Music" while the other would sing out the majestic strains of the "Pilgrim's Chorus."

... The lights were turned out in the compartment after we left Dijon. We had to get up early the next morning and it was a good idea to get a few hours' sleep. Soon heads began to lean to one side or the other and snores could be heard between the dull thud of the pistons and the regular panting of the locomotive.

Did Ruth go to sleep immediately? I have no idea, but I do know that I didn't fall asleep for a long time. Her head leaned gently in my direction, and mine, in a reverse movement and very slowly, leaned toward hers. Soon her hair was touching my cheek. I didn't dare move. I had not been this happy for a long time and I went to sleep, her cheek against mine, pervaded by the warmth of a friend, a sister, and a mother...

December 10, 1977

The peace initiatives are going to bring to light the hidden contradictions of our society: the will to reach a settlement, certainly, but also territorial ambitions; the will to compromise, but also the belief in a particular and decisive right to the land of Eretz Israel; the will to return to normal, but perhaps also an inability to accept what is normal.

I think I became aware of these difficulties as soon as I returned to Israel in 1967. It took me a long time, however, to admit that a living community follows paths that are often impossible to predict and map out in advance, that dilemmas and contradictions are part of this journey, that at best the role of each individual remains to affirm certain principles that are essential to him, in an attempt to erect dikes along the shores and guardrails along the edges of history.

I understood, little by little, that here one's gaze could not linger on the mere surface of things, that everyday problems were often far removed from the underlying rhythms marking our lives. I recognize the danger of this twofold perspective: it allows errors, and even aberrations, to be minimized in the name of a latent meaning; and it sometimes leads to committing these very errors themselves by using hidden norms as justification. Perhaps what we have to do is face the challenges of every day as though they were the only meaningful thing, but at the same time live the other dimension of things, as though daily life were of no importance . . .

Gradually the very look of places came to me to reflect this constant duality. When you enter Jerusalem from the plain, dilapidated districts greet the eye: on one side of the road, long rows of buildings obstruct the view of the hills; on the other, about a hundred yards away, the smelly little streets of the main market of the Jewish city open out before you. And as soon as you pass beyond the walls of the Old City, the glaring advertisements for Coca-Cola, Kent, and Assis assail you on every hand. Advertisements and filth. The Via Dolorosa is nothing but a commercial street of the Middle East in which the great black wooden crosses slowly borne along by groups of pilgrims during the Christmas season or Holy Week almost disappear amid the brightly colored crowds of tourists. Gimcracks and cheap junk reign everywhere, it would seem, everywhere the commercialization of the sacred seems to have emptied the sacred of its substance. This, at least, is your first impression.

But there is another Jerusalem, too: here something ungraspable seems to emanate from the stones, the hills, the light, the wind. Here things have a way of "being" that transforms everyday events into a shadow play against a background of immobility — of eternity, I almost said.

A way of being of things, and sometimes of people as well. The children of the old Jewish quarter, for instance . . . In the little sunny squares, between the synagogues and the reestablished rabbinical schools, they wander about in groups, deep in interminable discussions in which, I am sure, the assignments of the Yeshiva alternate with the complex rules for the exchange of marbles. Sometimes they throw themselves into games that to me are incomprehensible, secret. Their presence, evident everywhere, always seems incongruous to me in this setting. Incongruous but reassuring. For in the face of the past, of inflexible tradition, of a routine that is centuries old, and here suddenly reimplanted, they signify not only acceptance and continuity but also an uncontainable force, that of the present moment, that of life.

Other encounters come to mind. When you leave the Old City by way of the Armenian quarter, for instance, and take the street running along the Wall, where the arches, supported on blind façades, cut the burning pavement up into great patches of shadow, you can see monks clad in long black robes, their heads covered with pointed, vaguely terrifying hoods, walking along the walls in the most perfect silence. Try to see the look in their eyes: you will discover the immobile face of time.

Confronted with this weight of the ages, mingling ceaselessly with the familiar rhythm of everyday life, I have thought that perhaps in this place death, too, becomes more natural. Perhaps here it is consistent with the slow accumulation of things, with the bluish light of the air, with the subtle mixture of spicy odors from the Arab market; a necessary, almost imperceptible break; a leaf falling, a door closing, a footstep retreating . . .

That is how I perceive the other face of Jerusalem today.

At the end of November 1947, the United Nations General Assembly voted for the partition of Palestine into two states, one Jewish and the other Arab. In Jerusalem and Tel Aviv there was dancing in the streets; among the Habonim, horas lasted till dawn that Sunday. A few days later, fighting broke out with a vengeance. In the spring the tension became unbearable. In my far-off high school, I felt the breath of an epic spirit.

"A people cannot receive its state on a silver platter." This sentence of Chaim Weizmann's inspired one of the most famous poems of this period. Its lyricism may seem excessive and somewhat maudlin today, but this is precisely the way people felt and lived events during the months that I am speaking of. Natan Alterman's poem speaks of a boy and a girl, two of the hundreds who fell during those decisive days:

Then the nation, in tears and ecstasy, asks: "Who are you?"
And the two softly reply:
"We are the silver platter on which the Jewish state is offered you."

They so said and fell at its feet, enveloped in shadow.
And the rest shall be told in the annals of Israel.

How could one think of anything else, how could one live any other adventure?

From then on, I spent all my pocket money on newspapers, and thus, by comparing news stories, by reading all the commentaries, I managed, day by day, to follow developments on the battlefront. Confusedly at first, but then with growing conviction as the weeks went by, I felt that my place was no longer at "H IV." What was to be done?

I had made up my mind at the beginning of April. But the Habonim refused to arrange for me to leave for Israel: I was too young! I changed my birth date thanks to a few drops of ink eradicator, adding two years to my age, and joined the Betar, a youth movement with ties to Menachem Begin's Irgun.

One clandestine meeting followed upon another: "What do we want?" "Both banks of the Jordan!" My replies made a good impression and I was made a Beitari. In Paris, as in Eretz Israel, things were happening fast.

The headquarters of the Irgun for operations abroad were situated in the French capital, and it was there, within this group that had become almost autonomous, that the most daring and most irresponsible plans were hatched. Hostile to any sort of partition of Palestine, the Paris group dreamed only of fighting for the conquest of the whole of the historic homeland, even at the price of opposition to the nascent state. Arms, combatants, ships were needed. In the spring a first ship was ready; the French government would furnish the arms and permit about a thousand men to assemble near Marseilles.

On Friday, May 14, 1948, at four o'clock in the afternoon, David Ben-Gurion proclaimed the creation of the State of Israel in the great hall of the Tel Aviv Museum. The next morning the Arab armies attacked. The Irgun ship had to depart, whatever the cost.

On Thursday, June 3, when I returned to Henri IV after a brief visit at my guardian's, I found a message waiting for me: rendezvous the next day at 1800 hours, Gare de Lyon, for the train to Marseilles.

I was scheduled to take the written exam for the baccalaureate ten days later. I did not hesitate: I would be at the rendezvous the next day at 1800 hours.

The essential reasons for this decision were clear; they had to do with the events in Eretz Israel, my recent new awareness of their meaning, the excitement of the moment. But perhaps there were other factors, other nuances. For I could not forget the long idle Sunday afternoons when there was no meeting or demonstration and my schoolmates all joined their parents or friends of long standing. I would stop by my guardian's for a few minutes and then aimlessly roam the streets. Sometimes I would spend hours on a bench in some square, waiting for something, anything, to happen. I then began to understand clearly what I had previously experienced only passively: I was all alone in the world. People often told me I looked sad. I wasn't really sad, but I would sometimes fall into a sort of depression, and even though my plans for the future were apparently clear-cut, as the baccalaureate exams approached I began asking myself, more and more often, what was going to happen to me. To leave for Eretz meant merging my personal fate with a common lot, and also a dream of communion and community; it meant dissolving my personal anxieties in the enthusiasm of a group. For better and for worse, thus movements grow that sometimes change the course of history.

I warned my guardian not to expect me that Sunday. Another letter, which was to be delivered after my departure, informed him of my decision:

When you receive this letter, I will have already left Paris . . . for Palestine. You may be surprised, but don't worry: I am with a group of Beitarim and safe and sound. Above all, don't call in the police or any other organization of that sort; it would only cause you extra trouble and it would be useless, for when this letter reaches you I will already be on the boat.

Don't worry about what my uncles will say, for I'll be with them before you've written to them, and I'm sure they won't be all that unhappy with me . . .

As far as practical matters are concerned, I've taken all my underwear and my gray and beige suits, and the leather jacket, with me in my knapsack. Before I left I took the yellow suitcase, my briefcase, and my textbooks to a classmate who will bring them to you as soon as possible. Just in case, this is his address: . . .

I would also like to ask you to send word to the lycée that I am leaving the school and will not be taking the baccalaureate exams. Then everything is taken care of.

I will send you a long letter when I get there; I would have very much liked to say goodbye to you and thank you personally for everything you've done for me, but I was afraid you might do something to stop me from leaving. In any case, please don't think I'm ungrateful. Until I see you again in Palestine, I embrace you affectionately

Paul

P.S. (very important). Will you please pay my boarding fees for the third quarter, because otherwise they won't give me back a pair of sheets, two shirts, two shorts, and two pairs of socks that are at the lycée.

On June 5, the principal of the school wrote to my guardian:

Sir: I regret to inform you that your ward, young Friedländer, a boarder in section 1A, suddenly left the lycée yesterday afternoon at 4:30 p.m., taking advantage of the departure of the day students.

On our inquiry, it was discovered that he intends to join the Jewish forces in Palestine.

You will excuse my reminding you at the same time that the April–June term has not yet been paid for.

Yours sincerely,

P. Camenen, Principal

As far as the date and the hour of my escape were concerned, the principal was well informed; as for my objective, he was also correct. All that remained for me to do was, literally, to put to sea without let or hindrance.

How free and happy I felt as I walked down the rue Montagne-Sainte-Geneviève with my knapsack on my back, that Thursday, June 4, in the late afternoon! The great adventure was beginning.

It almost ended half an hour later at the Gare de Lyon. From the bulletin board of arrivals and departures I discovered, to my stupefaction, that there were three trains leaving for Marseilles a few minutes apart, on three tracks a long distance away from each other. Where should I meet the group? I was suddenly frightened. I couldn't go back to the lycée: any moment now, my escape would be discovered, and my *bac*, for very good reasons, would be seriously compromised. What was I going to do, since I didn't know the place where everyone was to rendezvous in Marseilles and didn't have either a ticket or a sou in my pocket? I decided to post myself at the gate to the platform from which the earliest train, the one at 5:50, would be leaving, and then run to the next platform, and if necessary to the third one. On the second platform I recognized a member of the group.

When we woke up, dawn had broken and there were olive trees along the tracks. Soon I spied the Rhône and the majestic outlines of the papal palace. Two more hours and we would be in Marseilles. And at this point my memory once again plays a curious trick on me. I remember the details, but the essential thing escapes me: when did I finally first catch sight of the sea? The thing I had waited for so long, so impatiently, had come to pass at last, but I don't have the least reminiscence that preserves this first encounter — unless my disappointment is expressing itself as a total memory block . . .

Our arrival at Saint-Charles and the hustle and bustle of the station: buses were waiting for us. We crossed the city and were on our way again, down the highway. But not for long this time. Soon came a tree-lined entrance, a gate, long rows of tents, a blue-and-white flag: our camp. Groups of curious bystanders greeted us on our arrival: our future traveling companions.

On June 11, at dawn, a long line of trucks pulled out. Destination: Port-de-Bouc. We arrived at the dock. Our boat was a Liberty ship, one of those that transported Allied troops during the last years of the war. We made out the name: *Altalena*. Those of us who knew the history of Zionism recognized the nom de plume of Zeev Jabotinsky, the founder of the movement we belonged to; most of the others, myself included, saw in it only a nice-sounding name.

Dozens of crates were piled up on the dock: arms and ammunition of all sizes and calibers. The longshoremen, Moroccans for the most part, refused to load them; they had guessed that this ship, bearing a Panamanian flag of convenience, was about to set out for the Jewish state. What did it matter! Military trucks arrived: the French army, with our help, loaded the ship. Then we went aboard, one national group after the other. There was another brief wait, and then suddenly there were sirens hooting, water seething, the rhythmical shuddering of the deck and the surge of the sea.

The previous evening I had written to Madame de L. and her husband:

Dear Godfather and Godmother,

I apologize for being obliged to confront you with a big surprise, but when you have read this letter you will understand that I couldn't say anything beforehand.

By the time this note reaches you, I will already have left France for . . . Palestine. I can understand your surprise. Who could have expected it? Certainly not me some time ago, but recent events have awakened a feeling in my soul that had been dormant there for a long time, the feeling that I was Jewish. And I want to prove it by leaving to fight alongside all the Jews who are dying in Palestine . . .

3

When the *Altalena* left Port-de-Bouc, the first truce of the Israeli-Arab war had just taken effect. Sending in reinforcements was now illegal. So getting this ship under way amounted to a daring step on the part of the Irgun command in Europe. In Israel, the organization accepted the fait accompli, and as the days went by, the expected arrival of the ship and its load of war matériel aroused growing excitement. For David Ben-Gurion's provisional government, on the other hand, this was an act of defiance, a provocation, and perhaps — who could tell? — the beginning of a plan for armed secession by the most extreme sector of the country. Countermeasures were called for. And so, when we were still off Rhodes, an entire brigade of Israeli army forces took up positions near Kfar Vitkin, around the dunes to which I would soon be stealing off to read Fromentin: the order was given to take possession of the ship, by force if necessary, when it arrived.

The hurried meetings we managed to overhear, the remarks exchanged here and there with the officers, the vagueness of the daily communiqués made us feel ill at ease, but no one foresaw the drama that was about to unfold. Struck with wonder by the sea, our heads full of our dreams, we spent the first days of the voyage on deck; despite the stifling heat, we talked long and hard in the bright light of this June solstice.

I was the youngest of the 940 passengers. I soon made friends. One of them was an American, Jim; the other, whose name, as I remember, was Ray, was English. Jim had fought in the Pacific and Ray at Arnhem, with the First Airborne Division. Two non-Jews come to fight for the rebirth of Israel!

Jim called me "the professor," and Ray, adding a qualifying adjective, "the little professor." They were both part of the group of veterans in charge of defending the ship when it set out for Tel Aviv after leaving Kfar Vitkin. It was there, I was told, that Jim was killed. One of our twenty dead. A cannon shot had set the ship on fire, and as men jumped overboard and swam toward the shore, the firing continued. This was the end of the *Altalena*.

For a few months the inhabitants of Tel Aviv could contemplate the blackened hull of the ship from the esplanade on the seafront: for swimmers it became a stopping place, a resting place, a place to dive from. By searching thoroughly, one could sometimes still find a blackened rifle in the hold and carry it off as a souvenir. And then the wrecked vessel was sent to the bottom or sold for scrap, I don't know which, while along the shoulder of the road to Jerusalem, the charred remains of the trucks became monuments to memory . . .

December 27, 1977

Christmas has gone by unnoticed; I scarcely took the time to watch the rebroadcast of the midnight mass from the Grotto of the Nativity for a few moments on television, and Christmases of other days scarcely came back to my mind.

This story is drawing to a close and once more the question arises: have I succeeded in setting down even so much as a tiny part of what I wanted to express? As a matter of fact, this quest, this incessant confrontation with the past during these months, has become sufficient reason in itself, and a necessary undertaking. And the words of Gustav Meyrink leap to mind once more: "When knowledge comes, memory comes too, little by little . . ." — a sequence, however, that has been inverted here: when memory comes, knowledge comes too, little by little . . . "Knowledge and memory are one and the same thing."

The problems that surround us, the problems of this country are with us still. These pages are ending while everything is still uncertain. For the first time, it is true, we see a possibility of peace dawning, but nothing is certain. For the first time the end of the tunnel seems to be in view, but there are those who consider the light glimpsed in the distance a dangerous mirage.

For several days now, people's euphoria has been waning and what is clearly a growing sense of unease is taking hold. More than once these days I have come to ask myself if a unique chance is not perhaps about to escape us. In an effort to clarify the essential, without confusing it with the meanders of the circumstantial and ephemeral, I have done my best in these pages to avoid any sort of strictly political reflections. It is nonetheless true that political decisions now dominate our lives and will determine the future of all of us. If we must one day take up arms again, not to defend what must be defended at all costs, but because we will not have been able to accept compromise at the proper moment, what today is only a temporary situation will have then become the very essence of the gravest of dilemmas, the very essence of tragedy.

But beyond these reflections on the immediate future, the uncertainty that now envelops us takes on another meaning and another dimension. It has always represented our manner of existence in the world, and in many respects, for better or worse, it has made us what we are. Sometimes when I think back on our history, not of these past few years, but rather its entire sweep, I can make out a perpetual movement back and forth, a search for roots, for normality and security, forever threatened down through the centuries, and I tell myself that the Jewish state may perhaps be only a step on the way of a people whose particular destiny has come to symbolize the endless quest — ever hesitant, ever begun anew — of all mankind.

Though we lingered for long moments on the deck dreaming and talking, we had other tasks as well: the usual duties — peeling potatoes, cleaning, washing dishes — paramilitary exercises, and above all, getting the arms and ammunition in working order, toiling for hours and hours in the compartments of the hold below deck, naked as galley slaves but full of endless enthusiasm. I became a specialist in cartridge belts for Spandau machine guns: nine ordinary bullets, one tracer bullet; nine ordinary bullets, one tracer bullet . . . I put thousands of them together this way, one after the other, and I confess I found pleasure in handling these arms and this ammunition.

In Prague, a single-seater fighter plane, painted in the most impressive camouflage colors, had been installed in a park (or was it on one of the city squares?), and you stood in line for hours for the right to get a close look at it or, supreme happiness, to sit in the cockpit as though you were the pilot. This first contact of my life with a war machine dates from the summer of 1938. Then in May 1940, as I have recounted, we had the chance to inspect light tanks when convoys going to the front halted near the children's home.

The crews would take a few minutes off to rest, have a drink, and smoke a cigarette. We youngsters could sniff the strong smell of leather, stroke the breeches of the machine guns, dream of battles: battles won . . . And in Néris, as the reader will remember, I had an imaginary machine gun mounted on the roof. What would be the outcome of battle this time?

One afternoon the alarm sounded. The ship began to turn in circles, faster and faster, and a sun that was already low in the sky began to circle faster and faster around the ship's rails. A boat was lowered with a few men armed with rocket launchers and depth charges. A submarine, doubtless an Egyptian one, had been sighted in the vicinity. An attack of this sort, I must add, had been feared from the beginning of the voyage: the *Altalena* had become the target of the British, the Arabs, and even our own Israeli army; an opportunity not to be missed . . .

The lifeboats could hold four hundred passengers. I could only hope that on this "little ship" of the children's song the youngest passenger would not be sacrificed . . . Soon order was reestablished: the alert had been for nothing, and from now on, it was thought, we had only to avoid the truce patrols in order to arrive at our destination without mishap.

My father's suits and his leather vest were in my knapsack; on my wrist was the most precious memento of all, a Schaffhausen watch.

In Néris, on Sunday mornings, I would sometimes come sit on my father's bed before he got up. He would pick his watch up off the night table and hold it to his ear for a long time, and then slowly, almost religiously, he would wind it. Once more he would listen to its secret ticking, and satisfied only then, it would seem, that he had properly carried out the ritual gestures, he would put the watch back on his wrist.

Sometimes we would go to the forest of Commentry to gather mushrooms. Standing very straight in his green overcoat, my father would walk ahead, parting the branches with his cane. Sometimes he would lean over and feel around in the moss, and we would discover chanterelles or a boletus. At regular intervals he would pull up the sleeve of his overcoat with his free hand, examine the watch, put it to his ear, and then our walk would be resumed.

At the hospital in Montluçon, after my father had telephoned to Saint-Béranger for someone to come get me and then rejoined my mother and me, he had strolled nervously up and down the room, and every few minutes, without realizing what he was doing, I imagine, as he continued to talk to me without a pause, he would look at his watch, this same watch. I have never met the person who sent it on to me, a Jewish doctor from Sens. Shortly after the war he mailed it to me at Saint-Béranger: my father and he had been shut up in the same freight car on the train taking them from Drancy to the east. The doctor had decided to try to escape; it was then that my father gave him the watch to send to me. The doctor jumped out of the train; the wheels passed over him and he lost both legs. He was picked up and survived. That was how the watch had come to me. I never took it off. One morning, as we were nearing the end of our voyage, I noticed that it wasn't on my wrist. One of my traveling companions had undone the strap and slipped it off while I was asleep. I searched for it and asked around, to no avail. There was no way of recovering it. Thus the most beloved memento of my childhood disappeared at the moment that I was approaching Israel, at the dawn of a new life. Symbolically, what measured time past was no more; symbolically, everything was beginning all over again.

The last two days of the voyage, we were no longer allowed to stay on deck: the *Altalena* was now a peaceful cargo ship. We maneuvered, and on the night of June 20 we arrived off the coast, but since an American ship had been sighted in the vicinity, we zigzagged out to sea again; this made a goodly number of us in the hold seasick. The next evening, we went inshore again. Around four o'clock in the morning, we were given permission to come up on deck.

There submachine guns stood pointing toward the sea every twenty or thirty yards. Men were on guard all around the ship. Did they know what was going to happen, or was it a routine precaution? I couldn't say. Jim was there, behind one of the guns. He whispered to me, "Hey, professor, everything okay?" But I was thinking neither of Jim nor of the others just then. Like everyone else, I was waiting.

The only sound was a very faint lapping of the waves, and the engines belowdecks also seemed to be turning over very quietly: the ship was gently gliding toward the coast. A few scattered coughs broke the silence. Then, off the bow, the sky paled and the first light of dawn revealed the outlines of dunes and orange groves. Out of the darkness there loomed up before us the land of Israel.

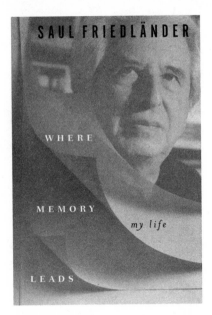